G000141662

Conversations and the Human Experience

Conversations and the Human Experience

A Self-Instructional Program to Improve How We Talk to Each Other

Selma Wassermann

ROWMAN & LITTLEFIELD
Lanham • Boulder • New York • London

Published by Rowman & Littlefield
An imprint of The Rowman & Littlefield Publishing Group, Inc.
4501 Forbes Boulevard, Suite 200, Lanham, Maryland 20706
www.rowman.com
86-90 Paul Street, London EC2A 4NE, United Kingdom

Copyright © 2022 by Selma Wassermann

All rights reserved. No part of this book may be reproduced in any form or by
any electronic or mechanical means, including information storage and retrieval
systems, without written permission from the publisher, except by a reviewer who
may quote passages in a review.

British Library Cataloguing in Publication Information Available

Library of Congress Cataloging-in-Publication Data Available

ISBN 978-1-4758-6753-4 (cloth) | ISBN 978-1-4758-6754-1 (pbk.)
   | ISBN 978-1-4758-6755-8 (ebook)

Horsie Bay
When I saw him there
In the middle of the road,
I shouted SIMON
with such authority
that hot dogs came to a halt
midway between plate and mouth
at Troll's sidewalk Eatery.
I grabbed him into my panicky arms
and held him there
for my own safety's sake.
A hundred reproaches telegraphed from my brain
and died there
behind compressed lips.
The words came out erect like small soldiers
From a long-term depository that stores what I know
And I spoke with pounding heart into the small of his ear,
Oh, Simon.
Grandma got so scared. "Please don't go into the road with-
out taking my hand."
It takes only two generations to learn to talk to children.

Contents

Preface

His tires screeched as he brought his Harley to a sharp stop at the driver's side of my car. His face aflame with rage, he knocked on the window and I opened it to his fury. "You cut me off, you (bleep) idiot!" His manner was menacing and I was stunned by such unleashed anger.

"I'm so sorry," I countered. "I really didn't see you and I am so very sorry."

My admission of guilt seemed to have struck him momentarily speechless and he sat back on his ride and tried to decide how to respond. There was an uncomfortable silence and then he finally said, "Well, don't do it again!" And he rode off the moment the light turned green.

Conversation, the way we talk to each other, is the essence of human experience. We humans are gifted with language—the very endowment that differentiates us from other species. And the ways in which we use and abuse language identify us.

For example, accents, according to Shaw's expert on phonetics, Henry Higgins, give clues to where we were born and raised. Certain words and phrases betray not only our origins but also our country, our social class, our generation, our "tribes." "I'm going to the loo," is typically British, as is "lift" for elevator, and "porkies" for lies. Floridian Bill uses "Y'all" when he means "you" and eats "grits" for breakfast. Canadians interject "eh" frequently at the end of their sentences. Neologisms invade our speech regularly; "meh" and "duh" have recently been added to the OED and "Google" has become a verb.

Different cultural groups often have their own ways of communicating with each other that reveal which group or clan they belong to. An earlier generation of youth used "hip" to signify "with-it-ness." Today it is more common to hear "cool" that encompasses more than just "it's okay." East Los Angeles habitués have their own argot, some of which may be undecipherable to others not of that area or generation. "Waasappining," "get yo head faded," "on the nickel," and "I feel you" may sound like a foreign language to those outside the area, but they communicate quickly and directly, connecting those on the "inside" to each other.

Some politicians make use of "spin" to give bad news a more positive twist. Calling the January 6 attacks on the Capitol "legitimate political discourse," attempts to persuade us that the riots and violence were reasonable protests. There are some TV "newscasters" and Internet sites that use disinformation to spread lies and conspiracy theories to convince viewers to take sides on important issues.

Because "free speech" is a cornerstone of our constitutional democracy, we have the right to protest, to make false statements, to say whatever we want, no matter how ridiculous or offensive, with little risk of being held to account. Social media, for example, is one venue in which it is possible to accuse, to vilify, to shame, to lie outrageously, without having to take responsibility for what we have said.

On the other hand, "political correctness" has, to some extent, muzzled "free speech" in some classrooms to accommodate those students who have a vested interest in certain topics of discussion. A Florida governor has been leading the charge to restrict what teachers can say and discuss in class relative to topics that include race, racism, gender, and certain history events. In fact, his executive order set new rules banning certain topics not only in schools but in the labor practices of private companies (Strauss and Bever, 2022).

This too has implications for how we talk to each other.

Even the briefest study of how humans use language will reveal what is obvious: Words have power; they have power to assault, to diminish, to inflict pain, to befuddle, to condemn, to persuade, to propagandize, to incite a riot, to sell you a device that you really don't need, to foment revolution. Cannily used they may convince you that down is up, that the sky is falling, that ivermectin is an effective COVID treatment. Goebbels, the Nazi master of propaganda, said, "If you repeat a lie often enough, people will believe it and you will even come to believe it yourself."

Communist leader Mao Zedong, in 1966, called on the nation's youth to purge the traditional elements of Chinese society of "old customs, old culture, old habits and old ideas," giving rise to the Cultural Revolution. His words resulted in a massive youth mobilization, the formation of the Red Guards, that closed schools, burned books, and carried out brutal attacks against the elderly and the intellectual population as well as destroying historical relics and artifacts and ransacking cultural and religious sites.

On the other hand, words have power to encourage, to inspire, to educate, to inform, to motivate, to placate, to amuse us, to satisfy, to cultivate our best angels. "We have nothing to fear but fear itself," President Roosevelt told Americans as he rallied a nation terrorized by the attacks on Pearl Harbor in 1941, when the United States was on the brink of World War II. Famous speeches throughout history have inspired us and are remembered for their stirring call to endure. "Give me liberty or give me death," "I have a dream," "Ich bin ein Berliner," "Ask not what your country can do for you; ask what you can do for your country."

Despite the importance and the widespread use of language as our primary means of human connectivity, there are few, if any courses at any level of schooling that aid and assist us in using language more intelligently—to communicate thoughtfully what it was we intended to say, to respond to others who count on being heard, to build respectful and caring relationships with each other.

There are no courses that demonstrate how some words are hurtful to others; how they may be helpful and enabling rather than dismissive; how they are consonant with what we had hoped to say. Perhaps that is one of the underlying reasons for "miscommunication" and for the breakdown of trust in our relationships.

All too often, words fall from our lips when we put "our mouths into gear before we put our minds into action." All too often the words we use may be inconsistent with what we had meant to say. Responding "off the cuff," without thoughtful appreciation of what we say and how we say it may produce statements that are not logical, that may incense rather than mollify, that may confuse rather than illuminate, that may be garbled rather than clear. They may not be respectful or helpful in the ways they respond to others, whether they are our children, our students, our friends, or strangers who approach our car windows. They may be hurtful instead of comforting.

David Brooks (2022) has alerted us about the ways we are now talking to each other: "It's not just normal bickering; there's a common desire to pummel, to shame, to ostracize others over disagreements that suggests something more fundamental than just minor differences in points of view." Anger and grievance seem, these days, to be at the root of the ways in which we are communicating with each other—especially those who do not share our beliefs. Sometimes a dialogue can seem so bizarre it feels as if we are trapped in conversation purgatory.

This book is intended to raise awareness of the ways we talk to each other—whether it be teachers talking to students, parents talking to children, adults talking to other adults. It would not be an exaggeration to claim that effective communication builds trust in human relationships—not a small benefit to raising awareness and improving skill in this human dimension of our lives. In today's culture, where trust is so grievously lacking in the ways we talk and respond to each other, this is hardly a small advantage. It is to that end that the materials in this book are offered.

Acknowledgments

I wish I could claim that I was born with the ability to use the kind of words in conversations that inspire inform, motivate, and encourage others as a genetic endowment. Alas, that was not the case; learning to use language facilitatively came as a result of serious study and application with several of my mentors in the educational process.

To each and all of them I owe a great debt; their teaching, guidance, and wisdom enabled my growth in awareness of my own conversational style, as well helping me to develop the skills used to facilitate the growth and enabling of others. I cite, particularly, the teachings of my primary mentors in this field, Louis E. Raths and Ed Lipinski, who were not only exemplars in their own conversation styles, but also gifted and patient teachers.

To these I must also add the early works of Charlie Truax, Bob Carkhuff, and Bernie Berensen, whose books in the field of human relationships were beacons that guided my own professional development.

To my wonderful family, who support and encourage me in my writing endeavors, I couldn't do it without you: dear departed Jack, daughter Paula, grandsons Simon and Arlo, and my three adorables: Maya, Kai, and Ruben. And not least, to my publisher Tom Koerner and the editorial staff of Rowman & Littlefield, my warm thanks and grateful appreciation for all you do to propel my work from manuscript into the marketplace.

Introduction

The octopus lay in the corner of the glass-enclosed tank, one tentacle tapping against the window. Craig stood there mesmerized, the eye of the marine animal catching his own, as if in private communication between them. Octopus and third grader locked in some silent relationship, each unable to withdraw from the spell that bound them.

The rest of the class had already moved on, and when the teacher looked back, the distance between the group and Craig had widened. She called out to him, "Craig, we're moving on. Can you catch up?"

Reluctantly he separated himself from the glittering eye, moving slowly to where the rest of his class was waiting.

"I wuz watchin' the octopus, Ms. Lee. He was movin' his arm to the window as if he wanted to touch me. He's got those suckers on those long things and I think he wanted to grab me and squeeze me. I wuz scared, but maybe he only wanted to be friends with me."

Which one of a dozen or more responses should Ms. Lee make to Craig? How will that response affect Craig's appreciation for this marine animal? For the sea creatures? For his attitude toward school and his teacher? For his interest in marine life? For the miracles of biology?

These are some of the questions that inform the ways in which teachers choose to respond to students.

Grandma has been left in charge of her four-year-old grandson at the pool. His lips have turned blue and she is worried that it is now becoming too cold to stay in the water. She calls out and tells him his time is up and he needs to get out. He grumbles and gripes his indignation, but she is adamant and insists. Like swimming through glue, he oozes his way out of the pool, reproaching her: "I thought grandmas were supposed to be nice, not mean."

Which one of a dozen different ways of responding will Grandma choose in replying to Arlo? What response will communicate to him her concerns about his health and safety? Which will address his sense of being treated badly? Which will ensure his continued positive relationship with his grandmother?

These are some of the questions that inform the choices adults make in responding to children.

An interviewer (Lyall, 2022) raised questions to fourteen "independent voters" to voice their concerns about President Biden's first year in office.

> Interviewer: If you could speak directly to the president, what would you tell him?

> Jules: I don't care about COVID anymore. I want my kids to have a regular life. I don't want the masks. I don't want them social distancing. I do not worry about them getting sick.

Which one of a dozen different ways of responding should the interviewer choose in replying to Jules? What response will ensure that the dialogue is kept open? What response will avoid putting him on the defensive and making him angry? What response will communicate respect for his position? What response will open his mind to alternatives?

These are some of the questions that inform the choices people make in responding to each other.

The words we use to talk to each other have power. They have power to hurt; to break down relationships; to cause a loss of trust. Some are so powerful that they may undermine a person's sense of self.

A teacher unknowingly may respond to Craig dismissively:

> Craig, you are holding us all up. The whole class is waiting for you. That's pretty thoughtless of you.

A grandmother unwittingly may respond to Arlo dismissively:

> That's too bad. I'm the boss and I say you need to get out of the pool right now.

An interviewer may unwittingly respond to Jules dismissively:

> You can't mean that! You actually want your kids to be exposed to COVID? You don't care if they get sick?

The words we use have power to encourage, to support, to show that you understand where the other person is coming from. These words can be so powerful that they may contribute to building more trust in human relationships.

A teacher may respond to Craig additively:

> Craig, I know you are very interested in that octopus and would love to stay there longer. But there are other things in the aquarium that I'm sure you would like to see too. Won't you please come and join us?

A grandmother may respond to Arlo additively:

> Oh dearest, I know you would love to stay in the pool longer, but I am so worried that you might catch cold from getting a chill. So won't you please come out now.

An interviewer may respond to Jules additively:

> You are pretty upset about the restrictions that COVID has placed on our lives. You want things to return to normal. You are worried about the effect that the restrictions are having on your kids.

Whichever ways teachers, parents, and other adults respond, these chosen words have power for them. A response has power to hurt or to help. It has power to be psychologically additive or subtractive, to empower or disempower, to enable or diminish the other. Responses can be inviting, appreciative, respectful. They can be rejecting, cruel, punishing. They can foster autonomy or they can cultivate dependency.

Perhaps this seems like overegging the pudding, assigning too much weight to statements people make to each other in human discourse. Of course, no one is going to die from a single hurtful response. Yet, any of us who has been at the butt end of sustained, cruel, punishing, and hurtful statements dished out by thoughtless and insensitive adults (or children) will know the power of such statements to diminish us. After long exposure to such responses, we begin to believe less of ourselves, that we are "bad," that we "will never learn," that our questions are stupid, that we are unworthy, that we are unable to do things for ourselves.

These negative feelings about self do not come from the ether. They occur as a consequence of significant adults' disrespectful, hurtful, and diminishing responses to who we are and what we do.

WHAT'S THE GOOD OF IT? (IT'S NOT ABOUT THE CHEESE)

"In our anger filled age, when people shop, travel or cope with some mild disappointment, things can get ugly real fast," writes Lyall in the *New York Times* (2022). She suggests that in our present situation, "things feel broken," the mood of shoppers "angry, confused, and fearful." The man in the market in Minnesota had asked for a type of blue cheese, which, he was told, was not available.

His demands became excessive, insisting that the clerk search in the back of the store, or look it up on the computer. And then "he lost it"—went out of control, exploding in a temper tantrum. The clerk, wise beyond her years, said, "I don't think this is about the cheese" (Lyall, 2022).

It is not only COVID and Omicron that have brought about this sense that our lives have been upended. So much is now uncertain; schools have been on again, off again, with respect to students returning to classes. Companies are undecided about when employees may return to the office. News from "informed" sources about whether we are now safe enough to eat in our favorite restaurant, or whether we need to "mask up" in enclosed public places seems to change from day to day; and if we go out to eat, can we be sure that the people at the next table have legitimate vaccination passports?

Anti-vaxxers and anti-maskers are active and vocal, stirring up further worry of being at risk even in small groups. The feeling of being unsafe among such uncertainties has wreaked havoc with our sense of security. The disharmony on the political scene has not only caused a rift between parties but has hardened into actual hatred. Reports from informed sources like the International Institute for Democracy and Electoral Assistance added the United States to its list of "backsliding democracies" (Homans, 2022)—suggesting the acceleration of the erosion and disunion of American democracy.

All of this unease is fomented by the steady stream of disinformation and blatant lies perpetrated by some TV newscasters, and social media sites on the Internet, contributing in a large part to our polarization and the unkind ways in which people treat each other.

In the words of the shopkeeper in Minnesota, "when people have to meet each other in transactional settings—in stores, on airplanes, over the phone—they are devolving into children, giving people license to act out."

It is far from a panacea to consider that certain human interactions may contribute to a sense of security, of calmness, of safety, but it is a powerful first step in addressing what is being presented by such large swaths of adults and children who are stressed beyond what has been endurable for them. It is a powerful first step to communicate to others that we have heard them, that we are appreciative of their situation, of their concerns, of their frustrations. It is a powerful first step to have the skills that enable us to make a personal connection with those children and adults who seem in jeopardy of coming apart.

What if? What if more adults and more young people were able to call on some interpersonal skills that gave them the means of responding to those presenting their angst, their concerns, their worries, their sadness, their lack of faith in their abilities to confront the difficulties that face them? What if more adults and young people could respond to others in a genuinely helpful, caring, thoughtful, responsive way? What if more people had the skills to make human connections healthier, more respectful, more responsive to what is being presented by another?

Would it make the world a better place? Would it put an end to the stresses and the discomforts so many of us are facing in these turbulent times? Hardly. There are no easy answers, no quick fixes, no panaceas for problems that seem insurmountable. But what such skills can achieve is to give us the means to make a human connection with others, to demonstrate caring, concern, and respect. They can work to create better relationships, building a spirit of connection between people.

Is that enough? For many, it is hardly debatable. Because communication that leads to improved understanding is preferable to communication that leads to conflict. Because helping is preferable to hurting. Because connecting with others builds trust and disconnecting leads to chaos.

HOW THE BOOK IS ORGANIZED

Learning to respond with respect and understanding to others is the primary objective of this book. It is aimed at teachers, parents, and other adults, whether they are talking to children or to each other. The materials included offer a self-instructional program in what are considered the essential elements of building effective and trusting relationships with each other.

The first section of the book introduces key interpersonal communication skills that, like a carpenter's tools of the trade, make for more effective interactions with others, be they students in a classroom, children in a living room at home, or adults in conversations with each other. The "tools of the trade" of the effective responder include: listening and attending skills; selecting appropriate responses; learning to listen to self in the process; freeing oneself from the need to make judgments; learning to become non-defensive in responding; using questions selectively.

The second section of the book includes a program of self-instructional activities that have been designed to elevate awareness of these skills, as well as promote skill development in these areas of expertise.

The program materials come from the author's long-term work at the university and in the field, teaching and training adults and children to use effective interaction skills to the benefit of all those in their realms of experience. They are offered to readers in the hope that they may develop greater expertise in building better human relationships in whatever field of endeavor in which they live and work.

PART I

The Essential Components of Effective Human Interactions

Chapter 1

Listening

"Tuning In"

Don't interrupt when people are talking!

Who me?

Listening skills are probably the most underrated in human discourse. Just because we "hear" doesn't necessarily mean we listen—that is, taking in fully, apprehending, tuning in to what is being said. "Hearing" doesn't mean that we have appreciated the words, the deeper meanings, the nuances, the implications. It doesn't mean that we have discerned the body language that either betrays or supports what is being said. In other words, learning to listen is more than just hearing. It is an acquired skill that opens the door to effective conversations, to meaningful connections with others.

The literature on counseling and "helping" is rich with references to the art of listening. In fact, what people say and how they say it tells us a lot about them, how they see themselves, and the world around them. They are the richest source of information that enables us to understand what is being communicated (Carkhuff, 2000).

"Active" listening (Fisher & Ury, 2012; Zenger & Folkman, 2016; Kyle, 2014) is something that many people have not learned to do. For many of us, listening is no more than waiting until the other person finishes, so we can get our chance to speak. Active listening demands a great deal more. It demands active engagement in the process of tuning in, not just passively "receiving." It is a matter of striving to comprehend the meaning of what another person, adult or child, is attempting to reveal to us, a sharpened awareness of what the other person is trying to convey (Combs & Snygg, 1951).

In order to do that, to be able to extract meaning from the totality of what a person is presenting, in words and behavior, whether it be your neighbor, your student, your sister, your toddler beginning to form words and sentences, there are a few a priori considerations that enable that process of "tuning in."

At the very first, the good listener must show, in their face, their eyes, and in their body language that they are present—that is, they are giving their full and undivided attention to the speaker. Making that kind of contact communicates that presence and is evidence to the speaker that the listener is ready to tune in, to understand what is being said.

Friere (1983) calls this presence, "attending"—the taking in and the making meaning of the totality of what is being expressed.

A second factor in the act of active listening is the ability to free oneself of the rush to judge. Too often when we hear another's statements, we are too quick to have a response that agrees, that criticizes, impales, mocks, evaluates—that is to say, we put ourselves in the position of judge and jury. There is no quicker way to terminate an open discussion than to issue a judgment on it.

How does one do that? How do we free ourselves from the quick rush to judgment? It helps when we focus on attending –the act of tuning in and being present to another's statements, clearing the mind and being open to what is being said, to focus on "being present" as the other person is speaking.

A third factor in active listening is to refrain from interrupting. Too often in human conversations, we listen, and as we are listening we are already forming an opinion of what is being said and how we are going to reply. We can't wait until the other person is finished talking. We want to get our two cents worth in too!

Learning to wait, to listen to the full commentary, takes a bit of self discipline. Once again, tuning in and being present as we listen to the other person helps us to wait; we are taking the full measure of what is being said, both in words and in behavior.

This is especially difficult when the other person is making a statement that has high emotionality—words that cut into the heart of what the listener believes or cares deeply about. When such statements are forthcoming, it is a good idea to be prepared, to breathe in, and concentrate on listening and giving one's full attention to what is being said.

Perhaps it was Carl Rogers (1965) in those earlier days of the "client centered therapy" movement who introduced us to the need to become "active listeners" in our communications with others. He suggested that to become an effective listener, that is, to be able to put ourselves into the position where we can free ourselves from judging and listen fully to what a person is telling us, getting at their meaning so that we have heard and understood, is a learned skill.

So, active listening, focused, comprehensive, and strategic, requires discipline. A wide spectrum of messages can be conveyed through spoken communication, and the shades of meaning can be very subtle. Great concentration is needed to absorb, organize, and store verbal communication in a form that makes later retrieval both possible and useful. But if true communication is to occur, then it is essential to acquire perceptive listening skills (Leonard, 1991).

What then are the key conditions for active listening?

KEY CONDITIONS IN ACTIVE LISTENING

What follows are not necessarily the "ten commandments" that make a person a good listener. But they are, at the very least, those conditions that are basic to effective interpersonal communication. In the demonstration of these conditions, listeners show themselves to be present, to be tuned in, to be fully on-side with the other person in the conversation. You don't have to say, "I'm here. I'm listening." You show that in your behavior:

- Make and hold eye contact with the other person (child or adult).
- Tune in to what is being said. Be naturally interested.
- Show in your body language that you care about what the other person is saying.
- Discern the tone of voice, the nuances of expression.
- Look for evidence of any affect (verbal or nonverbal).
- Be aware of indicators of stress being revealed.
- Avoid interjecting your own idea in response to what is being said. Don't interrupt.

- Take in (apprehend) the full meaning of the other person's statements.
- Make it safe for the other person to present his or her ideas.
- Free yourself from the need to judge the other's ideas, either in word or tone. (Wassermann, 2017)

DEVELOPING ACTIVE LISTENING SKILLS

Learning any complex skill is a not a task for cynics or defeatists. While learning to become an active listener is not in the same league as mastering Bach's Cello Concertos, it does demand what learning other skills demand: that is, beginning with an understanding of the what, practicing the how, making continued self-assessments of one's practices, and making improvements based on those assessments. None of this is mastered in a day. Each requires a commitment to engage, to practice and use the skills, and most important, to develop a critical awareness of what is coming out of one's mouth in the act of speaking.

It is not unlike learning to listen to oneself playing music: tuning in to "hear" if there are any wrong notes, being non-defensive in admitting to them, and making a strong effort to correct those wrong notes in the next practice session. That is the way we learn to improve musical artistry; that is the way we learn to improve active listening skills.

Part II of this book offers a developmental set of self-instructional practice tasks—not unlike "finger exercises"—that enable skill development in the several key components of effective communication. A set of these is devoted to practice in developing active listening skills.

Chapter 2

Responding

Teacher, can I go to the bathroom?

But you just went a few minutes ago.

Mom, I can't find my other shoe!

You're always forgetting where you put your things. I'm not your maid.

(Neighbor to neighbor)

I'm sick and tired of being cooped up. I've got cabin fever.

Stop complaining. Other people are worse off than you.

There are dozens of possible responses we make as we listen to others—whether they are children or adults—and those responses carry a lot of weight in both the negative and positive sense. In choosing to respond to statements or questions, we have "n" options. Responses may give information:

How can I fold this origami pattern?

First, you fold the top down, like this. Then you fold the sides over, like this. And then, pull the entire piece inside out! And voila!

They may be confrontational:

Ruben, stop kicking that chair leg! If you do it one more time, you will have to go to your room!

They may be judgmental:

How did you like the article I wrote for the magazine?
It certainly stirred up a lot of feelings in me.

They may be directive:

Clean up your room right now, Ethan, or there will be consequences!

They may foster independence:

I see you are having trouble figuring that out. But I'll bet you can find a way to do it.

They may be cruel and punitive:

You're eating a second helping of pie? You are going to bloat up like a whale.

They may make you feel liked, accepted, and understood:

Can I play with you guys?
Yes! Great! We were hoping you'd join the team.

I forgot my lunch.
That's okay. I'll share mine with you.

In whatever ways people respond to each other, those responses have power. A response has power to hurt or to help. It has power to be psychologically additive or subtractive, to empower or disempower. Responses can be cruel, punishing, and rejecting. They can foster autonomy, or they can cultivate dependency. They can open lines of conversation, making personal connections to others, or they can create barriers between people.

The bottom line in selecting how we respond to others is to know which responses are respectful and genuine; which foster our personal connection; which attend wisely to what is being communicated. And uppermost is our ability to be authentic in making those responses.

THE OVERARCHING CONDITION OF RESPECT

No matter the situation, no matter the context, the beginning point of responses that contribute to improved human connections is respect. That has to go to the top of the list of how people respond to each other. Whether interactions are from adult to child, or adult to adult, no matter the age, communicating respect for them opens the door to improved human connections. "Even toddlers deserve to be treated with respect" (Lansbury 2022).

Respect is communicated in the ways we listen to others (see chapter 1). It is communicated by our focused attention to what the other person is saying. It is communicated in our expressed interest, both in our words and in our behavior. It is communicated by our authenticity in making our response.

It is communicated by not interrupting, giving the other person a chance to complete his or her statements; by refraining from making critical judgments. It is communicated by our genuineness in what we say and in tone of voice; by refraining from using clichés (I feel your pain; I hear you); by our willingness to put ourselves in the place of the other—"walking in their shoes"—as they tell us what's on their minds. How we communicate to others reveals how we view them.

This is easier done when the playing field is less emotional, when we have less vested interest in what is being said or done, when we are freely able to be neutral. This is more difficult when the issue is "hot," when we do have vested interest in what is being said, when the statements being made are "trigger points" that set our teeth on edge.

Learning to be in control of all of that is not easy; but the first step is being aware of those trigger points and keeping those feelings under control, while we make every attempt to listen, to understand, and to respect the ideas, the positions, the arguments of another. It is a practiced behavior and one that is learned over time. But without the ability to do that, the effects are more than likely to sever human connections than build them.

To behave in ways that are truly respectful of others and their ideas takes a predisposition to the idea that others deserve respect.

SELECTING APPROPRIATE RESPONSES

Choosing appropriate responses begins by knowing about the kinds of responses that contribute to opening a dialogue without "baggage." That is, responses that are clearly respectful and that are free of signs of emotionality.

Added to this is how we use these responses appropriately in conversation. This is a learned skill; we become more proficient the more it is used and the more we are able to reflect on and hone those skills. As we grow more adept, we become more non-defensively aware of "what is coming out of our mouths." We are able to listen to ourselves as we are speaking.

To open those lines of communication, and to respond in ways that build trust, several kinds of responses meet those criteria:

Paraphrasing

On the surface, paraphrasing responses may seem bland, colorless, and perhaps ineffectual. But history of their use is a strong indicator that they have power to communicate to others that their ideas have been heard. They also "say the idea back" in some new way, reflecting the idea in a verbal mirror, so that the other person has an opportunity to "hear" it from a fresh perspective. A paraphrase response doesn't challenge; it is an indicator that the statements expressed have been heard. It is probably the safest type of response that can be made among the repertoire of responses and one of the strongest to build trust in human relationships. Paraphrasing responses include:

- Saying the idea back in some new way
- Interpreting the idea

Although it does not meet the criterion of paraphrasing, another helpful response at this "basic" level is asking for more information. For example, "Tell me more" or "Help me to understand what you mean." Underlying this response is the suggestion that you are interested and want to give the other person a chance to elaborate, to make his or her ideas clear to you.

An example of how a teacher uses these "basic level" responses in a graduate class discussion about the film *The Miracle Worker* shows how these responses illuminate the big ideas of the film (i.e.,"the power of a teacher to make a difference"). Note that the only question used is the one that asks for more information. Note, too, the respect shown in the teacher's interactions with the students.

Teacher: What are your thoughts on how this teacher influenced her student's life?

Kim: She was able to take the girl, Helen, from a borderline existence into a world where she could communicate with others.

Teacher: You see Helen as initially in a borderline existence. (Paraphrases)

Kim: Yeh.

Teacher: Tell me a little more about that, Kim. (Asks for more information)

Kim: Well, I think that without the ability to communicate you can't be a part of this world. You can't communicate with others. They can't communicate with you. You are living a marginal existence.

Teacher: Without the ability to communicate you are hardly in the world. (Paraphrases)

Kim: Yeh.

Noreen: Can you imagine what it must have been like for her? Helen? To be trapped without the means of telling anyone what she thought or felt? A terrible prison-like existence. Worse.

Teacher: She didn't have the ability to tell what she was thinking or feeling. She was in a terrible trap. (Paraphrases)

Noreen: No wonder she was wild. Her behavior was wild. Her frustration must have been unimaginable.

Teacher: So much frustration; it produced her aggressive behavior, which her parents saw as wild. (Paraphrases; interprets)

Noreen: The frustration-aggression theory.

Teacher: You've read about that. (Interprets)

Ross: That's the gift of that teacher. Annie Sullivan. She gave Helen the gift of communication. In this case, the gift of life.

Teacher: What she gave Helen enabled her to break out of that trap. (Interprets)

Ross: Without it, she would have been doomed. But it sure wasn't easy.

Teacher: Helen didn't make it easy for her. (Paraphrases)

Ross: Not Helen. Not the parents.

Teacher: Annie didn't seem to have much support for what she was trying to do. (Interprets)

Ross: I don't know how she did it.

Teacher: She had a lot of courage. (Interprets)

Ross: Beyond belief. I don't know if I could have stuck it out.

Teacher: Sometimes, the gifts teachers give take a lot of courage. Annie never seemed to lose faith in herself. (Paraphrases; interprets)

Jennifer: It seems to me that teaching requires courage. Teachers do give gifts, but these are not easy to deliver. And sometimes they are not even appreciated.

Teacher: Teachers have gifts to give but giving them is not easy. They have to work hard, sometimes against all odds, to give those gifts. And sometimes, they are not even appreciated. (Paraphrases; interprets)

Jennifer: It would be nicer if they were appreciated more.

Teacher: There's some sadness in your voice when you say that, Jennifer—like teaching can be a thankless profession. (Interprets)

Jennifer: Sometimes I think it is.

Joan: It may be sometimes. But look at the gift Annie got in return for what she gave.

Teacher: Say a little more about that Joan. (Asks for more information)

Joan: The satisfaction. Can you imagine the satisfaction that Annie felt when Helen made that breakthrough?

Teacher: There's nothing quite like that feeling of satisfaction—to know you made a profound difference in someone's life for the better. (Interprets)

Joan: I guess that's why we want to become teachers. I think that drives us all to teach.

Teacher: So teachers give gifts, but we are gifted in return. These are the rewards of teaching. (Paraphrases)

Joan: You bet. (Wassermann, 1994)

Janine, age eleven, has come home from school and told her mother that she was now "nonbinary" and that her mom should no longer refer to her as "her," or "she" but "them" and "they." While her mother is, at first, nonplussed by this news, she tries, in her interactions, to be respectful of her daughter's position, as well as to elicit more information about her ideas. At the very top of her agenda is to not alienate her daughter and to communicate that she wants to understand. She avoids questions that may appear to interrogate and instead relies on the basic paraphrase responses throughout.

Lin (mother): I'd really like to know more about how you came to that decision. (Asks for more)

Janine: Some of my friends and I talked about it. We think that it's better.

Lin: This is a better idea—not to use "she" or "her" in talking about you. (Paraphrases)

Janine: Yes. Because of how that makes you feel.

Lin: When you say "she" or "her" it makes you feel a certain way. (Paraphrases)

Janine: Yeah.

Lin: Can you tell me a little more about how those words make you feel? (Asks for more)

Janine: Well, I think there is some bad stuff about calling girls "girls" and "she."

Lin: I wonder if you can tell me more about the kind of bad stuff that you are describing. (Asks for more)

Janine: I think that it means that girls are less important than boys. I think it's a kind of put down for girls.

Lin: I'm going to use a big word to try to describe what you are telling me. You see those terms as a form of discrimination against girls. (Interprets)

Janine: Yes, that's it. I don't want to feel that I'm less than boys. I want to feel the same.

Lin: You'd like to know and feel that you are equal to boys. That boys and girls are equal.

Janine: Yeah. We're different, of course. But we should have the same treatments. Not be different because of our sexes.

Lin: Boys and girls should be treated equally. And you think that using more gender neutral words to refer to girls will help. (Paraphrases)

Janine: Yes, I do.

Lin: I appreciate your telling me this. And I will try to remember to use those gender neutral words from now on. I may forget, so I'm counting on you to help me remember.

A journalist approached one of the truckers whose vehicle was one in the convoy that had blockaded the border crossing between Windsor, Ontario, and Detroit, Michigan. She wanted to write about some of the motives that the truckers had for their protest. She knew that feelings were high, and that she needed to be respectful of points of view that might be very different from hers in order to try to make sense of their ideas. It was not her intention to try to persuade anyone, but only to try to discern what motivated their actions.

With notebook in hand, she asked one man, Mr. Lewis, if he would be willing to talk to her about what was behind his protest.

Lewis: We just want to live the way we lived before and be proud Canadians, but right now we can't be.

Reporter: Can you tell me more about what you mean, about how you can't live the way you lived before? (Asks for more information)

Lewis: Well, it's about our freedoms. We want our freedoms back.

Reporter: There are more restrictions on your freedom. (Interprets)

Lewis: Yes, there are. All those masks we have to wear now.

Reporter: The masks you have to wear are an infringement on your freedom. (Paraphrases)

Lewis: Yes. That's true. And you shouldn't have to wear them. You should have a choice. That's freedom.

Reporter: So freedom means you get to choose if you wear a mask or not. (Paraphrases)

Lewis: Yes. This is a free country. You should not have these laws imposed on you.

Reporter: In a free country, you should have a choice as to whether you wear a mask or not. (Paraphrases)

Lewis: And you should have a choice if you are going to get vaccinated or not.

Reporter: So your choice should extend to whether you get the vaccine or not, too. (Paraphrases)

Lewis: Yes. That's right.

Reporter: You seem to be pretty firm in your beliefs about your freedoms to choose, about whether you need to wear a mask and whether you get the vaccine. (Interprets)

Lewis: Yes, I am.

Reporter: You are so determined in your beliefs that you wanted to become part of this protest, to create a blockade of trucks to show where you stand. (Interprets)

Lewis: Yes, and I'm going to be here until they give in to our demands.

Reporter: Can you tell me something about the demands? (Asks for examples)

Lewis: Well, Mr. Trudeau needs to be a man of the people. To understand how we feel.

Reporter: I see. Thank you, Mr. Lewis.

Arlene and Sally are neighbors who have lived in the same suburban neighborhood for many years. Although they are "good neighbors" they hold very different political, social, and economic points of view, so these are topics they try to avoid when talking to each other. Arlene is mindful of her "trigger points" when talking to Sally—and today those points have been intensified by Sally's seemingly irrational statements about conspiracy theories. Because she knows she has a hard time trying to be neutral in her responses, Arlene chooses another approach.

Uppermost in her thoughts is that she does not wish to alienate her neighbor, nor to make "bad friends" with someone she has to live next door to, and perhaps even come to her to borrow a cup of sugar.

Sally: Of course I'm not getting the vaccine. I know for a fact that if you get the vaccine there's a microchip implanted in it and it will be used to spy on us. We aren't safe. I read it on the Internet.

Arlene: I know you believe that, Sally. But I'm sorry if I can't share those beliefs. Could we talk about something else? I really don't want to quarrel with you. Okay?

END NOTES

Even a cursory examination of the examples of interpersonal responding emphasizing the use of paraphrasing will reveal several essential features. First is the obvious and overarching condition of respect that is prevalent in each response—whether it be teacher to students, parent to daughter, adult to adult. Second, there is the absence of judgment in each response. At no time does the responder use his or her position to criticize, to condemn, to agree, to affirm, to venture an opinion on what the speaker is saying or thinking.

Third, the reader will note there are few questions raised in these interactions. While questions are discussed about their special uses in their own chapter, it is seen above that they are not necessary in getting to the heart of the other person's thinking, beliefs, ideas. In other words, paraphrasing does the job of contributing to sound, respectful, helpful, and fruitful interpersonal communication.

They are not the only ways in which responders can reply. But they, at the very least, open the doors to making those important interpersonal connections.

ONE FINAL WORD

There will also be times when other than facilitative responses are called for. Times when you are asked for information and can provide it gladly. Times when you think it's best to offer advice. Times when you want to share some ideas or anecdotes of your own. In other words, if someone asks you "how to find Fifth Avenue" the best response is to give directions. Inappropriate would be to paraphrase, "Oh you are lost." It is important to be sure that when you use paraphrasing responses they are appropriate to the particular situation. That too is a big part of your mastery of interpersonal skills.

Chapter 3

The Art of the Question

The first graders were having their daily "show and tell" at the beginning of the morning and it was Bobby's turn. He was describing a game that his grandmother had given him for his birthday and he spent several minutes trying to explain how it worked. His classmates were attentive and listened respectfully as Bobby attempted to draw a verbal picture of his new game. When he finished, he asked his classmates, as part of the process, "Are there any questions?"

Philip raised his hand and asked, "What's your grandmother's name?"

Questions are the building blocks of obtaining important information. They may aid us in seeking what we want to know, help us to understand the points of view of others, increase our knowledge base. While questioning is one legitimate form of obtaining information in an interpersonal dialogue, we do not learn this art from any serious study of questioning strategies during any part of the educational process. In most cases, we learn about questions from observing and absorbing the kinds of questions used by teachers, parents, news reporters on TV, and other authority figures.

It should come as no surprise, therefore, that the questions we use may be for better or worse; that they may reprimand, challenge, demand, insult, make us feel stupid. Cannily used, they may manipulate us to a particular point of view or action.

To study the art of the question is to learn that they are cunning little things. Depending on how they are phrased, on voice inflection or use of particular words, they may serve a higher purpose in making more positive human connections, or they may sever those connections as swiftly and as harshly as if they were blades of steel. Put in a certain way, they may challenge rudely, promoting anxiety and defensiveness on the part of the other person. Put another way, they may offer invitations to respond safely. A particular choice of words can fall, like concrete blocks, to crush an interpersonal dialogue. Another choice of words can electrify a discussion, charging it with power and energy.

Questions may focus on what is trivial and insignificant, concentrating the dialogue on small, irrelevant details. They may go after the "big ideas," illuminating significant and rich concepts. "Leading" questions may influence a person to accept a particular point of view.

Elevating questioning to an art in conversations is partly a product of one's ability to be aware of not only the kinds of questions that get at the heart of what we want to know but also learning how to best phrase them so that they are less intimidating, threatening, confrontational, intended to expose someone's lack of knowledge. The bottom line is that even the best questions are interrogations. That is why they are best used sparingly in interpersonal conversations, and with conscious appreciation of their power to intimidate.

QUESTIONS THAT SHOULD BE AVOIDED

There are several groups of questions that either should be excised from one's interpersonal discussions because they serve to put the other person, child or adult, on the defensive, intimidate, or even insult. For example, questions beginning with "why" more than often raise anxieties since they, from the moment they are spoken, create stress.

Why haven't you finished your homework?

Why is your room such a mess?

Why are you dressed like that?

Why aren't you wearing a mask?

Why do you believe all that disinformation?

Why did you do that?

Why are you being so stubborn?

These are but a few examples of questions that seem like interrogations and that, in ordinary circumstances, put a child or an adult on the defensive. On the surface, they are not intended to give information to the inquirer; they seem rather to be accusations disguised as questions.

If the aim in a conversation is to open lines of communication, such "why" questions should be avoided altogether.

Another group of questions that are best left unasked are those that Carkhuff (1969) calls "stupid." Stupid questions are irrelevant to the discussion; they are unnecessary interruptions to what the other person, child or adult, is saying. They indicate that the asker of the question has no real connection to what is being said. For example:

I'm really excited. We are planning to take a month's holiday in Hawaii. I'm going to have a real vacation in the sun!

Did you know that Millie went to Bermuda last year?

I'm having a lot of trouble with my math homework. I need some help!

What's your math teacher's name?

I read the reports of those people going nuts on the airplane. They were so disrespectful and some of them were even violent.

What airline were they flying on?

Stupid questions do more than disregard what the other person is saying. They are insensitive to what is being said, irrelevant, and disrespectful. They implicitly communicate that what the person is saying has no merit; the question shifts the focus of the conversation away from the other person's comments and ideas. They are anathema to the objective of building improved human connections.

A third group of questions that should be avoided are those that are laced with sarcasm, with inappropriate humor, with overt rejection, with negative judgments about the other person's comments, ideas, positions. At worst, such questions are so utterly destructive that those who experience a steady diet of them often carry scars long afterward. More often, they sound like reproaches:

How come you don't know that? Have you lost your ability to think?

It's green? You think it's green? How on earth did you come up with that idea?

What? You can't tell the difference between what is true and what is a lie? What's wrong with you?

How come you are having such a hard time making such an easy decision?

Questions like these are not intended to promote a dialogue between adult and child, or adult and adult. They are, rather, intended to criticize, to expose ignorance, to point out shortcomings. Few of us come away unscathed from such questions. For those who experience such questions, the result is likely to sever the interpersonal connection altogether. It is impossible to build trust in conversations when such questions as these are part of the interactive dialogue. It has been said that such questions are like "punching people in the face with words."

MORE PRODUCTIVE QUESTIONS

There's no argument that using questions thoughtfully, intelligently, and respectfully helps others think more intelligently about statements being made in conversation. Effective questioning may also add a dynamic quality to a conversation, charging it with positive energy that not only illuminates understanding but reveals the inquirer's deeper interest in what is under discussion. One of the keys to asking more productive questions is for the inquirer to be aware of the big ideas that are either implicit or explicit in what is being said. They rarely look for single right answers (e.g., Who wrote *Ulysses*?).

However, even more productive questions should be used sparingly, and with attention to voice inflection, nuance of statement, and the impact of the statement on the respondent, whether child or adult. As questions, they cannot refrain from being challenging, because they ask the other person to think more carefully about what is being said, about the issues under examination, about the validity of the statements. Too many challenging questions may be counterproductive; a few, put discreetly and sensitively, can move a discussion forward and open new doors.

To aid in the process of furthering examination, they should be clearly stated, sharply focused, inviting rather than intimidating, respectful of the other person's feelings and opinions.

Adult to adult: I'm stressed about having to prepare dinner for my in-laws. My mother-in-law is very critical.

Response: Making dinner for someone critical is stressful! Perhaps you can begin with an idea of what kinds of foods she likes?

Child to parent: I finished my homework. Now can I play with my tablet?

Parent: Can you tell me, before you go off to play, what your teacher asked you to do in that assignment?

Child: I don't understand why people would behave so rudely on an airplane.

Teacher: Can you come up with some hypotheses that might explain it?

Child: I don't know what we can do about all the plastic waste. We are drowning our planet in plastic.

Teacher: You're pretty upset about it. But perhaps you have some ideas for how we might go about reducing our own needs for plastic?

TURNING QUESTIONS INTO STATEMENTS OF INQUIRY

It is less intimidating for respondents to hear questions in a less confrontational, less challenging form. When questions can be put as statements, respondents do not have to wade through layers of mental anxiety before offering their responses.

For example, instead of asking, "What examples can you give?" an inquirer might ask, "You may have some examples to support our ideas." Instead of asking, "Is there an inconsistency between those two statements you just made?" the inquirer might ask, "Help me to understand. I'm seeing an inconsistency in your statements. Have I misunderstood you?"

Such differences are not so much differences in substance as in tone. Statements are less aggressive, less challenging, less confrontational, softer. They are more like invitations to respond than inquisitions.

In the examples above, another way of seeking that information may be put thus:

> I'm stressed about having to prepare dinner for my in-laws. My mother-in-law is very critical.

> Making dinner for someone who is so critical is stressful. You may have some ideas of the foods she might like.

> I finished my homework. Can I play with my tablet now?

> Before you go off to play, I'd like to hear a little bit about the assignment you did.

> I don't understand why people would behave so rudely on the plane.

> You may have some ideas to explain it.

> I don't know what we can do about all that plastic waste. We are drowning our planet in plastic.

> It's very alarming to you. And I'll bet you have some ideas about what we might do here at home, as a beginning.

Using more productive questions in an interpersonal discussion means being alert to how questions might impede, rather than promote ongoing dialogue. It means using questions sensitively and infrequently. It means being cognizant of how a question might impact the respondent. It means, once again, as in all other types of responses, that the asker is quite clear and fully cognizant of what is coming out of his or her mouth. But used skillfully, productive questions can shed new light on important ideas and move the conversation forward.

THE WELL-ORCHESTRATED DISCUSSION

It will be obvious from the reading of the last chapters that an interpersonal dialogue that builds trust, opens lines of communication, and enhances our human connections is not made up of a row of questions, or of any single set of statements. The well-orchestrated discussion is built on several components. At the very first, the responder must reveal that he or she is attending and listening to what is being presented. In addition, responses should always be respectful, and singularly appropriate to what is being said, as well as showing genuine interest in what is being said. Any trace of phoniness or artificiality immediately puts the kibosh on productive human connections. Questions should be used sparingly and when used, voiced in a non-threatening, non-challenging way. Responses that paraphrase should be the main avenue that drives the dialogue forward.

Conversation A: Adult (1) to Adult (2)

This is a particularly "hot" issue for Adult (2) who tries hard to keep his own feelings out of his responses.

> Adult (1): No, I didn't vote for Obama. I'm not prejudiced, but I was not ready to see a Black man in the Oval Office.
>
> Adult (2): You have no prejudices against Black people. (interprets)
>
> Adult (1): No. I just didn't want to see one for my president.
>
> Adult (2): You believe that a Black person is not fit for the presidency. (interprets)
>
> Adult (1): It's not that. It's just a feeling I have.
>
> Adult (2): Your feelings seem to be in charge of your decisions. (interprets)
>
> Adult (1): Well of course. My feelings are important.
>
> Adult (2): Thinking is important but feelings overrule them. (interprets)
>
> Adult (1): It's a gut feeling.
>
> Adult (2): It has nothing to do with being prejudiced. (interprets)
>
> Adult (1): I don't like to say I'm prejudiced. It's not something I'm willing to admit.
>
> Adult (2): Something about being prejudiced is uncomfortable for you. (interprets)
>
> Adult (1): Yeah. And I don't like to talk about it.

Adult (2): I understand. Perhaps you can tell me what characteristics you would look for in a presidential candidate? What are some of the attributes that would cause you to vote for that person? (raises a question to shift the focus of the discussion)

Adult (1): Well, I don't know off hand. But I think the person should be honest. And should be smart enough to take on the job. And maybe have some experience with running a country or a state. I'm not sure.

Adult (2): You haven't mentioned race as a factor in your choice. Is this not important to you too? (raises a question to connect what adult (1) is saying now to what he said before)

Adult (1): No, it's not important. That is, it shouldn't be important if the person is qualified.

Adult (2): The race factor is not important to you if the candidate is qualified in all the other areas you think are important. (paraphrases)

Adult (1): It shouldn't be important. But I think it is.

Adult (2): You are having some concerns about your ideas about a candidate. (interprets)

Adult (1): You are making me muddled up about it. I need to think about it some more.

Adult (2): I'm sorry. Perhaps we should stop now and give it a rest.

Conversation B: Adult to Pre-Teen Boy

Adult: You seem to be spending a lot of time on your tablet.

Boy: Yeh. It's my favorite thing.

Adult: It's something that gives you a lot of pleasure. (paraphrases)

Boy: There are so many games. I love working on the games.

Adult: The games are more than interesting. They also challenge you. (interprets)

Boy: Yes, they do. You have to think hard to figure out how you are going to respond.

Adult: They challenge your thinking. (interprets)

Boy: And you have to be quick about it too.

Adult: There's something about being fast to respond that is important. (paraphrases)

Boy: Yes. I'm getting a lot of skills when I work on my tablet.

Adult: Many skills are involved in what you are doing. But I'd like to ask a question if I may. When you spend so much time on your tablet, does this not take time away from playing with friends? (raises a question that opens a new line of inquiry)

Boy: Hmmm—yes, I think it does. But I'd rather play on my tablet than play with friends. Is that bad?

Adult: I can't answer that for you. It's something you decide for yourself. But I might ask if there are any consequences to spending so much time on your tablet, with less time spent on playing with friends. (puts a question in the form of a statement to ask for consequences)

Boy: I don't know. I guess I'm just a kid who would rather play alone than with a group of other boys.

Adult: Playing on your own, on your tablet, is more satisfying. (interprets)

Boy: It is for me. I guess that says something about me, eh? (Laughs)

Conversation C: Teacher to Grade 4 Student

Teacher: You seem to be having a lot of trouble with your math assignments.

Student: I'm not good at math. I never was good at math.

Teacher: Your math work has been a problem for you for a long time. (paraphrases)

Student: Yes. I'm good at other things. But not math.

Teacher: And that seems to be a worry for you. To not be good in math. (interprets)

Student: I'm afraid to say it.

Teacher: It's more than a worry. You don't even want to talk about it. (interprets)

Student: It's because my teachers in my other classes thought I was dumb.

Teacher: Some teachers might have thought you were not smart because math gave you so much trouble. (paraphrases)

Student:Yeh. And I got embarrassed. Every time I got my paper back I was ashamed.

Teacher: I can understand that. It was embarrassing for you to have those bad marks. (interprets)

Student: Sometimes I wanted to cry. Sometimes I just wanted to run away and hide.

Teacher: Hiding would have protected you from that embarrassment. (interprets)

Student: I wanted to run away from school.

Teacher: It hurts deeply when you can't get good marks on your school work. It's more than embarrassing. It's humiliating. (interprets)

Student: I wish I never had to do math. If I could only do reading I'd be okay.

Teacher: You do well in reading and perhaps that's your favorite subject. But math is a big problem. (interprets)

Student: Do you think I'm dumb?

Teacher: Heck, no! That's the last thing you are. (responds genuinely to student's question)

Student: So how come I can't get the right answers on my math work?

Teacher: Perhaps it's because there's something that is standing in your way from figuring it out. Perhaps like a mental block? (interprets; raises a question that shifts focus of discussion)

Student: Can someone have a mental block and not be dumb?

Teacher: Of course. It's a teacher's job to help you lift that mental block. Some teachers can do that for you. (responds genuinely to student's question)

Student: I'd like to try. I'd like to do better in math.

Teacher: I'll see what I can do to help you. Would that be okay? (responds genuinely to student's concern; offers help if wanted)

CONCLUSION

The above examples of conversations show how the use of paraphrasing, interpreting, and infrequently used questions can open doors in building our human connections. Even a cursory glance reveals that each response, in its own way, is an invitation to reply. At times responses may lead to new insights into what the respondent is thinking and saying.

These are, of course, learned skills; using them artfully, genuinely, and respectfully provides the "inviter" with important tools that enable and cultivate meaningful conversations. They give us the means to enrich our human connections.

Chapter 4

Once More with Feeling

Lucy: The doctor is in

Charlie Brown: I worry all the time. How can I stop worrying?

Lucy: Snap out of it! Five cents please.

It is inevitable that there will be times in discussions when a person, adult or child, will reveal some deep-seated feelings that are obvious or undercurrents to a conversation. The feelings may arise from some argument, from a slight, from an offense, from some frustration, concern, worry. In such instances, it is more helpful to respond in ways that show not only respect and genuineness, but also address those feelings.

When such responses can be used effectively, they offer support and encouragement. They serve to make a person feel more secure, less afraid, less alone. These responses require not only an understanding of what kinds of statements do this, but also the skills needed to speak them in caring, thoughtful, genuine, and respectful ways.

They require a person's ability to do more than listen. They require the ability to attend to the surface and underlying feelings being presented and to reflect them accurately. This ability to be empathic is a key ingredient in being able to connect with others humanly and humanely. Without the use of empathic responses, conversations may get stuck in the more cerebral realms and never get to the feelings that lurk behind the surface. The conversations remain one-dimensional.

The key to responding with empathy is how a person recognizes both the content of the message as well as the affect. This includes the ability to be aware of the shades of meaning as well as the more obvious verbal expressions. Often, such awareness and ability to respond in kind takes a while to master. And the route to that mastery lies in one's continued use of such skills with careful attention to the process as well as a heightened awareness of the effect of those responses on others.

To be avoided are trite responses that lack genuineness, such as "I feel your pain," as well as those that skirt or avoid the affect. Probing questions are singularly inappropriate in responding with empathy because they reveal a lack of understanding. Giving advice, when a person, child or adult, is baring his or her soul to you is not only not helpful, and non-empathic, but useless. We cannot ever completely put ourselves into the shoes of another and that is why we cannot advise, because we never have the full picture.

There are occasions when a person, child or adult, will share some of his or her innermost feelings when a listener replies, "Oh, that happened to me too." And thus the opportunity to provide empathy, to show that one understands the feelings of another, is defeated. Implicit in the listener's response is the unexpressed statement, "What you are saying has little importance to me. You should be listening to me instead."

The best empathic responses are those that show that we are attempting to understand, from the other person's perspective, what he or she is experiencing. Or as that five-year-old philosopher Charlie Brown put it: "It's great to feel understood."

A helpful way to begin teaching oneself to respond with empathy is by watching, and learning from people who are skilled in this process. In fact, children whose parents are well versed in the use of empathic responding will, by their daily exposure to these skills, learn from those primary experiences. Failing that, reading about how this is done by studying examples is second best—but not second rate.

Conversation 1: Adult to Adult

Adult (1): I don't know what to do about my dad. He's only eighty, but I think he is losing his ability to function on his own. And he is totally resistant to moving to a care facility. I worry about him all the time.

Adult (2): I can see how stressed you are. This is a problem that has been giving you some sleepless nights.

Adult (1): Oh yeah. How can you tell? Are my eyes so bloodshot?

Adult (2): I can see the signs of stress in your face and yes, your eyes look tired to me.

Adult (1): You know I've talked to him about moving to a place where he can be looked after. Where he can be safe. But he won't even talk to me about it. He shuts me down.

Adult (2): It's impossible to open the door to that issue when he won't even talk about it. And it is so frustrating for you.

Adult (1): What can I do? I'm at my wits' end with worry.

Adult (2): Your dad seems to be totally resistant to considering any options. And this is making you angry.

Adult (1): Yes, I'm so angry at him. I'm so angry at the way he is so closed down. I'm so angry at not being able to get him to see what he needs.

Adult (2): It seems to me that your anger over his lack of response is becoming paramount in your interactions with him.

Adult (1): Oh—I think you have just hit the nail on the head. It's my own anger that is making me crazy. It's getting in the way of my dealing with him in more appropriate ways.

Adult (2): Maybe you can give me some ideas of what you might consider more appropriate ways.

Conversation 2: Parent and Nine-Year-Old Child

Child: The teacher wants me to do it. And I'm scared.

Parent: Tell me what the teacher wants you to do.

Child: She wants me to stand up in front of the class and read my story.

Parent: That's a scary thing for you to have to do.

Child: The other kids will make fun of me.

Parent: You think they will laugh at you.

Child: Yes, because they're mean.

Parent: You are worried that the other kids are so mean and they will be mean to you.

Child: I don't want to have to do it.

Parent: The teacher is making you do it and that is making you feel worried.

Child: I wish I could do it. But I am afraid.

Parent: It's not only that you feel bad. It scares you to have to get up there in front of the others.

Child: Do you think it's because I'm stupid?

Parent: Oh my dear—that's so far from what I think. I think you are wonderful and special and kind and thoughtful, and I am so proud of you all the time.

Child: Oh. That makes me cry.

Parent: Sometimes you need to cry to let your feelings show.

Child: You don't think I'm a baby?

Parent: No, dearest. I think it's perfectly okay for boys to cry when they feel sad.

Child: You make me feel better. But I still don't want to do it. To stand up there in front of the class.

Parent: Maybe you and I together can figure out what you can tell your teacher.

Child: Okay.

Conversation 3: Professor and Graduate Student

Teacher: You were supposed to bring me the proposal for your thesis today.

Student: (Hesitantly) I haven't got it.

Teacher: Tell me about it.

Student: A couple of things got in the way. I wasn't able to finish it in a way that satisfied me.

Teacher: Life sometimes gets in the way of our other plans.

Student: Yeah (laughs). Actually, if I'm telling the truth here, I sat down and stared at the blank computer screen for hours. And nothing. Just nothing.

Teacher: The thought of putting some words down has defeated you. You are stuck.

Student: Yeah. And it makes me feel like a jerk.

Teacher: It may feel as if you are the only student in the world who is having trouble pinning down a thesis proposal.

Student: Is it because I'm not cut out for it? I'm worried that maybe I've bitten off more than I can chew.

Teacher: Right now it seems that the job of doing a thesis is more than you can handle. You are worried about your competence to carry it through.

Student: Yeah. I seem to get paralyzed when I look at the computer screen. Nothing, I mean nothing, comes out of my head. Like it's a big big empty space.

Teacher: Your fear of not doing it well seems to overpower you and it clouds your thinking.

Student: Does anyone else feel like this? Like they're too stupid to write a thesis?

Teacher: (Laughs) I think I've heard the same story several dozen times.

Student: I'm not alone? Others face the same hurdles?

Teacher: Join the crowd! It's a common feeling among graduate students who are just starting out. You are not alone.

Student: That makes me feel a little better—but I still need to find a way to overcome my stress about writing.

Teacher: Let's see if we can work out some strategies together to get you over this first hurdle. How does that sound to you?

CONCLUSION

There are dozens of studies that point to the effectiveness of empathic responses as a contributor to improved human relationships (Carkhuff & Berenson, 1967; Truax & Carkhuff, 1967). And these studies, as well, show that one can develop these skills by putting them into practice, becoming more acutely aware of how we are using them and their impact on others. Like the skills mentioned in the earlier chapters, empathic responses begin with listening and attending—tuning in to what is being said, how it is being said, and generating a response that attends to both feelings and content of the message.

Of all the other interpersonal skills used in our conversations, empathic responses probably carry the most "weight" in terms of their ability to convey to another, "I understand." And in terms of "weight," there are probably few greater conversational gifts that we can offer than our understanding.

Chapter 5

Caveats

When the Divide Is Too Great

There's nothing that dooms a conversation more than a person's lack of respect for another; a lack of awareness of the other person's situation and emotionality; a lack of regard for the conditions that are part and parcel of where the other person is "coming from." The interpersonal skills that have been presented in the former chapters provide some ideas on how these shortcomings can be addressed, and how certain interpersonal skills can contribute to improved human conversations and human connections.

However, all is not perfect in an imperfect world. Even for the most accomplished listener, there will be times when a situation is so fraught with high emotionality that it becomes impossible to use even well-developed interpersonal skills. Yes, we each have our own "trigger points" that make us go tilt in the face of statements that touch on nerves.

What's then to be done? How does one respond in the face of insults, of irrationality, of abuse, of statements that have no logic, that are aimed at our most vulnerable human facets? What's to be done when the divide is too great between what we are hearing and what we might say in response?

These are the most difficult situations, and the ones in which it may not be possible to even begin an effective conversation. Sometimes it's best to just walk away. In some cases, it may be a good idea to respond with, "I'm not able to talk about that right now." In some cases, one might say, "That's too hot an issue for me to talk about."

Withdrawing and not entering into what promises to be an uncompromising situation has a dual effect. It removes the onus from the listener of having to respond. Second, it prevents the conversation from escalating into a more unreasonable and more unreasoned realm. Sometimes it's just not possible to have a conversation when the person on the other side of the dialogue is beyond reach.

Withdrawing may be the best response—but even that should be done with a degree of respect and genuineness. Any response that serves to inflame an already "hot" situation may be more than counterproductive. It may be incendiary.

PART II

Skill Development Materials

Chapter 6

Introduction to the Skill Development Materials

The interpersonal interactions at the heart of human conversations described in the previous chapters of this book are rooted in the theory that the words we use in talking to each other have power. They have power to nourish, to add substantially to our human connections. They also have power to harm, to diminish our options for making those human connections. The words we use can communicate caring and regard. They can also belittle, ridicule, and reject. They can open lines of conversation and they can close them down.

While the first chapters describe the several important conditions by which interpersonal interactions can contribute to those positive connections, this second part offers a series of skill development tasks, that provide a sequentially programmed introduction to a person's growing mastery of those facilitative interactions.

The tasks progress *ad seriatim*, from the first steps of observing and analyzing different examples of facilitative interactions, and lead, eventually, to one-on-one practice. Like other skill development programs, the more one puts these skills into practice, with the concomitant component of reflection on practice, the more likely is it that slowly but surely, progress will be made toward mastery. Of course, none of this can be effectively done without the "person-in-training's" beliefs in the importance of mastering such skills and their willingness to devote time to master them.

While it is undoubtedly true that such skill development tasks are more effectively done with a partner, a buddy, a friend, a colleague, that is not an essential requirement. Working on one's own will also lead to substantial gains in one's mastery of facilitative conversation skills.

So, now, as the teacher said, we begin.

Chapter 7

Introduction to Facilitative Interactions

In this introductory task you will be studying some examples of inter-personal interactions and making observations of the ways in which the adult responds to the child or adult in the dialogue.

When you have finished studying the two sets of conversations, you are asked to respond to a few questions to focus your attention on specific components (i.e., what you see as the critical differences in the ways of responding), and also how the adult's response impacts on the child or adult at the other end of the conversation.

Note: In these self-instructional tasks, it is always preferable for two people to work together conjointly, to study, analyze, and share wisdom. It is also more pleasurable to work with a buddy. But failing that, good results can also be gained by solo study.

MATERIALS NEEDED

A way of keeping track of your responses—either in a journal or on a laptop or tablet. Either forms work—as long as you have an ongoing record of your work on these tasks. Use the "Analyzing Responses in Human Discourse" section at the end of this chapter to help pinpoint the kinds of responses being made in each conversation.

STUDYING THE CONVERSATIONS

Conversation 1: Teacher to Teacher (It's Driving Me Crazy!)

Betty: I'm at my wits' end. I really don't know what to do with him anymore.

Anne: Tell me what's going on. I want to hear about it.

Betty: It's Barry—that sweet kid in my Grade 6 class. I've tried everything but can't seem to find a way to help him.

Anne: I'd like to hear more about what he's doing and how that is frustrating you.

Betty: Okay. I'm getting ahead of myself. He's a nice boy, never have any trouble with him with respect to behavior. He does okay in reading, but where he just stumps me is in math. I can't get him past simple addition and subtraction facts.

Anne: His learning problems lie in math. But in other curriculum areas, he's doing okay.

Betty: You know, the other kids are doing long division and fractions and decimals. But Barry is struggling with adding $2 + 2$.

Anne: Even the simplest addition facts seem to defeat him.

Betty: Yeah. I'm lost!

Anne: You've tried many different strategies but nothing seems to be working.

Betty: I'm almost at the point of giving up. I tried using Cuisenaire rods, but he was embarrassed and said they made him feel like a baby.

Anne: Working with concrete materials didn't work. They made him feel like a first grader.

Betty: Yeah and that made me feel stupid and ashamed to have put him in that place.

Anne: Your lack of success with him is making you feel like a bad teacher.

Betty: Oh, you are so right there! It's not that I'm a new teacher. By golly, I've had several years of experience! You would think that I would be able to figure out how to help this kid.

Anne: It's not only that he continues to be unsuccessful in math; it's destroying your feelings of being a competent teacher.

Betty: You've got it! I am feeling stupid and incompetent. Something else I'm worried about is how this business of utter failure in his math work is doing to his overall sense of himself. I mean, if he feels defeated and I am not able to help him, what does this tell him about his sense of self-worth?

Anne: There's a double whammy here. On the one hand, Barry is losing out on math and is failing in that subject. On the other hand, you are worried that this failure is affecting his sense of self-worth as a learner.

Betty: You know, if math could be sports, he would shine! He's about the best sports player on the field! The kids all want him on their teams!

Anne: If only math were basketball! He would excel!

Betty: Maybe I could invent some math problems that centered on sports? What do you think?

Anne: Connecting math to sports—perhaps sports scores—you think that might be worth a try.

Betty: I had another idea when we were talking just now. What if I used money—you know, coins of different denominations, as manipulatives. That wouldn't have the onus of being babyish? What do you think?

Anne: It sounds to me as if you have a new idea of how to help him.

Betty: I'd like to give it a try. And another idea just came into my mind. But don't think this is crazy.

Anne: Tell me about it.

Betty: You promise not to breathe a word of this to a soul?

Anne: You don't have to worry about me.

Betty: Suppose when I marked his math papers, I erased the wrong answers and put in the correct ones? In that way, he would never get a bad mark on math. Do you think that's crazy?

Anne: It's radical, I agree.

Betty: Hey, I've got to get back to class now. Thanks for listening. And hey, stay tuned for the next chapter of my life with Barry. Sigh.

Conversation 2: Teacher to Teacher (It's Driving Me Crazy!)

Anne : I'm at my wits' end. I just don't know what to do with him anymore.

Vicki: What's going on?

Anne: It's Barry—that sweet kid in my Grade 6 class. I've tried everything but can't seem to find a way to help him.

Vicki: What's going on with him?

Anne: He's a nice boy, never have any trouble with him with respect to behavior. He does okay in reading, but where he just stumps me is in math. I can't get him over the simple addition and subtraction facts.

Vicki: Oh don't worry. Lots of kids have trouble with math.

Anne: But you know the other kids are doing long division, decimals, and fractions. And Barry is still struggling with simple addition and subtraction facts.

Vicki: Maybe he's got a math disability. You know, like some kids have reading disabilities.

Anne: Well, maybe that's the case. But that doesn't tell me how to help him.

Vicki: Maybe he needs a special assistance teacher?

Anne: Well, maybe. But heck, I'm an experienced teacher. I'm not a beginner. You would think that I could find a way to help him.

Vicki: What have you tried? Maybe your strategies aren't good?

Anne: I've tried to give him manipulatives. You know, I brought in some Cuisenaire rods. But he told me they made him feel like a baby. So that was a dead loss.

Vicki: That's bizarre. Why would they make him feel that way? Lots of older kids use manipulatives.

Anne: I don't know. Maybe he's seen them used in the lower grades?

Vicki: Maybe you should try to persuade him that they are not for little kids, that older kids use them?

Anne: I don't think that would work. I think it's a matter of his self-esteem.

Vicki: Oh, lots of kids that age begin to feel that way.

Anne: Every time I return his math paper, it's always with seven or eight addition and subtraction facts wrong out of ten. So each time he has to face his failure. And I feel so bad for him.

Vicki: Well, you can't fix what is broken. Maybe he just isn't a math kid. Maybe you have to accept that?

Anne: This is going to sound crazy to you, but what if I changed his math answers on his paper, erased the wrong ones, and put in the correct ones. Then he wouldn't get a failing paper back each time.

Vicki: Are you kidding me? That's just crazy! That's about the worst idea I've heard!

Anne: Well, maybe I'm at my wits' end after all. Maybe I'm just a bad teacher.

Vicki: Don't feel that way. Lots of teachers don't have success with every kid. You just have to accept that.

Thinking about Conversation 1

1. What are some general observations you made about Anne's responses in Conversation 1?
2. What are some general observations you made about Anne's responses to Betty in Conversation 1?
3. Make a critical analysis of the responses with respect to the following:
   - What kinds of responses did Anne use most frequently? (See "Analyzing Responses in Human Discourse.")
   - What was being communicated by those responses to Betty? How did you determine this?
   - What evidence in the dialogue revealed Anne's ability to "tune in" to what Betty was saying?
   - How did Anne's responses work to build trust in the relationship? How did you determine this?
   - What, in your view, is likely to be the long-term effect of Anne's interactions on Betty? How did you determine this?

Thinking about Conversation 2

1. What are some general observations you made about Vicki's responses in Conversation 2?

2. What are some general observations you made about Anne's responses to Vicki in Conversation 2?
3. Make a critical analysis of the responses with respect to the following:
   - What kinds of responses did Vicki use most frequently? (See "Analyzing Responses in Human Discourse.")
   - What was being communicated by these responses to Anne? How did you determine this?
   - What evidence in the dialogue revealed Vicki's ability to "tune in" to what Anne was saying?
   - How did Vicki's responses work to build trust in the relationship? How did you determine this?
   - What, in your view, is likely to be the long-term effect of Vicki's interactions on Anne? How did you determine this?

Reflecting on Interpersonal Facilitative Responding

1. What are some feelings you have in response to these two conversations? What did you like? Dislike? What made you feel comfortable? Uncomfortable?
2. Based upon your analyses, what do you consider to be significant characteristics of building trustful relationships in these conversations?

Conversation 3: Parent and Son (Report Card Blues)

Ian: Did you bring your report card home, son?

Charlie: Yes, Dad. It's in my backpack. (Reaches in) Here. Have a look. I hope you won't be disappointed.

Ian: I know you tried your best.

Charlie: I didn't do so well in Physics, as you see.

Ian: Yes, I see that. It's kind of a downer for you.

Charlie: Yes. It's my worst mark. I'm pretty cheesed off about it.

Ian: You've been having problems with Physics all semester.

Charlie: You know, Dad, I study hard. I really do. I get all my homework done on time. But whatever I do, I can't seem to satisfy Mr. Reynolds. His standards are too high.

Ian: I know you've been working hard. I see you at your desk every evening working on your homework. You are not a sloucher.

Charlie: Maybe Physics is just not my cup of tea. Maybe I'm too dumb to grasp those abstract concepts.

Ian: I understand that you would feel that way. But you know, Charles, that's not my impression of you. Being dumb is the last thing I would think about you.

Charlie: I appreciate that, Dad. So what do I do now? Do you think I should appeal the mark? It brings my grade point down. Do you think I should switch courses? Or perhaps ask for another teacher?

Ian: You've got several ideas for what to do next. First, you are worried about your overall grade point average. So maybe you are wondering if you should change courses or teachers.

Charlie: What do you think I should do, Dad?

Ian: That's a hard question for me, Charlie. Because I can't completely put myself in your shoes. I need to know how you feel about it. And whether you feel that improving your grade point is so essential.

Charlie: Well it certainly impacts on my college application.

Ian: So that's the essential issue for you. The college application.

Charlie: I wonder if you can have your college application accepted with a poor mark in Physics?

Ian: That may be something you want to investigate, at the very least, to calm your worries. Having done that, what might be some of your next steps? I'd love to hear what you have to say about it and how you might problem-solve it. And I'll be right here if you need to discuss it with me further or want help in clarifying your decision.

Charlie: Thanks, Dad. I really appreciate that you are not coming down on me for it and for being so understanding.

Conversation 4: Father and Son (Report Card Blues)

Stuart: Did you bring your report card home, Charles?

Charlie: Yes, Dad. It's in my backpack. I think you are going to be a little mad at me.

Stuart: Uh-oh. You'd better tell me before I get the bad news. What did you fail?

Charlie: I didn't exactly fail. But I got a low mark in Physics.

Stuart: Physics? That should be a piece of cake for you. How did that happen?

Charlie: I really don't know. I work hard. I do my homework. I think I understand what the teacher is saying. But I just didn't do well on the exams.

Stuart: Are you sure you are studying hard? And not goofing around? Physics isn't that hard and you are not exactly dumb.

Charlie: I don't know. When it comes to the test, I just freeze up. It's like I get so anxious I can't think straight.

Stuart: Listen, you've got to get over this. Being anxious before a test— everybody does that. You're better than that. Just force yourself to be calm and concentrate.

Charlie: I try, Dad. I really try. But it's just not working for me.

Stuart: I don't know what to tell you, but I can tell you this. This is definitely going to impact your college application. Because it's bringing your grade point average down.

Charlie: Don't you think I know that? And I'm really worried.

Stuart: I don't know why you have to spend so much time listening to that junk music and playing those computer games. Maybe you should have spent more time studying.

Charlie: I don't spend that much time on games. I really do study hard.

Stuart: I can't believe that. If you had studied hard you would not have gotten that mark.

Charlie: I can't seem to convince you that I really tried. I tried hard.

Stuart: If that were true, you would not have gotten a C. I'm really disappointed in you, son.

Thinking about Conversation 3

1. What are some general observations you made about Ian's responses in Conversation 3?

2. What are some general observations you made about Charlie's responses to Ian in Conversation 3?
3. Make a critical analysis of the responses with respect to the following:
   - What kinds of responses did Ian use most frequently? (See "Analyzing Responses in Human Discourse.")
   - What was being communicated by those responses to Charlie? How did you determine this?
   - What evidence in the dialogue revealed Ian's ability to "tune in" to what Charlie was saying?
   - How did Ian's responses help build trust in the relationship? How did you determine this?
   - What, in your view, is likely to be the long-term effect of Ian's interactions on Charlie? How did you determine this?

Thinking about Conversation 4

1. What are some general observations you made about Stuart's responses in Conversation 4?
2. What are some general observations you made about Charlie's responses to Stuart in Conversation 4?
3. Make a critical analysis of the responses with respect to the following:
   - What kinds of responses did Stuart use most frequently? (See "Analyzing Responses in Human Discourse.")
   - What was being communicated by these responses to Charlie? How did you determine this?
   - What evidence in the dialogue revealed Stuart's ability to "tune in" to what Charlie was saying?
   - How did Stuart's responses build trust in the relationship? How did you determine this?
   - What, in your view, is likely to be the long-term effect of Stuart's interactions on Charlie? How did you determine this?

Reflecting on Interpersonal Facilitative Responding

1. What are some feelings you have in response to conversations 3 and 4? What did you like? Dislike? What made you feel comfortable? Uncomfortable?

2. Based on your analyses, what do you consider to be the most negative characteristics of the responses in Conversation 4?
3. Based upon your analyses, what do you consider to be significant characteristics of building trust in these conversations?

CONCLUSION

As an introduction to the different ways of responding in conversations, you've been studying the four transcripts and making some analyses of how the "responder" in each serves to build trust in the relationships. You are also analyzing the different ways of responding that reveal how the responder "tunes in" and attends to the problem being presented.

Before moving ahead to the next task in your self-instructional program, you might want to check again to make sure you have understood the different ways of responding, how each response works to build trust in relationships, and how different responses affect the person on the other end of the continuum.

Below may be a helpful tool in identifying various types of responses that are "additive" or "subtractive" in human discourse.

ANALYZING RESPONSES IN HUMAN DISCOURSE

Responses That Diminish Trust

1. Doesn't give the "other" a chance to finish the statements
2. Shifts the discussion of the problem to the responder and away from the other person
3. Tells the other person what happened to him or her
4. Talks too much
5. Interrupts; cuts the other person off
6. Heckles, is sarcastic, belittles the other person's ideas
7. Shames, humiliates, is offensive in responding
8. Gives advice; tells what the responder did in a similar situation
9. Puts the other person on the defensive
10. Makes judgments about the statements or the person

Responses That Build Trust

1. Expressly reveals attending and tuning in to what is being said; expressly shows interest in what the other person is saying and feeling
2. Expressly reveals respect for the other person's statements/feelings
3. Accepts the other person's statements, no matter how off-putting they may be; doesn't make judgments about the statements or the person; is non-defensive in responding
4. Paraphrases the statements with accuracy
5. Makes effective interpretations of the statement
6. Asks for more information or examples to clarify a point being made
7. Is reassuring in accepting what is being presented
8. Shows confidence in the other person's ability to deal with the situation

Chapter 8

Practice in Choosing Appropriate Responses

In this task you begin your practice in the skills of attending, paraphrasing, and remaining respectfully neutral, first by identifying the nature of the original response and then by substituting one that is more appropriate in meeting the criteria above. Use the "Analyzing Responses in Human Discourse" section in chapter 7 as your guide.

In formulating your response, remember that:

- attending involves "listening" to what is being said and apprehending the full meaning of those statements.
- paraphrasing involves the ability to formulate a response that accurately reflects the meaning, by capturing the key ideas of the statement.
- being non-judgmental involves being respectful and attentive, without evaluating or judging, agreeing or disagreeing with the ideas, either in word or nuance of statement.

If possible, work with a friend or colleague in this practice task. Such collaboration allows not only for discussion before committing to a response, but also provides a way of making critical assessments of each other's responses. Such critical assessments provide each of you with a basis for making informed edits of your responses.

Record your responses in your journal, computer, or tablet, so you have an ongoing record of them.

PRACTICE TASK

1. In our country people are free to speak their minds but there are always consequences. If you say something offensive, you may have to bear the criticism.
   Response A: I don't think that's right. Sometimes there are no consequences to what you say. You can get away with saying anything you want.
   Your response: _____

2. People ought to learn to think before they open their mouths. Then we might have a more illuminating discussion, rather than just an exchange of ignorance.
   Response A: Are you saying that's what you think I do? Give me a break!
   Your response: _____

3. A few states have banned classroom discussions of controversial political and social issues. In states like Florida and Texas, teachers have already been fired. That makes teachers afraid of what they are saying in class. I thought we had free speech in this country!
   Response A: Teachers should be held accountable for what they say. There is no such thing as free speech in schools.
   Your response: _____

4. There's a lot of tension in our community around racial issues. I'm not sure how to address this with my neighbors.
   Response A: Just ignore them. You're not responsible for what they think.
   Your response: _____

5. Am I wrong in not wanting to return to work in the office, after I've been happily working at home for the last 18 months?
   Response A: If everybody felt that way, offices would close down. Do you want that?
   Your response: _____

6. My son brought home his spelling paper with half the words spelled wrong. I don't know how I can help him.
   Response A: Let his teacher handle it. That's her job.
   Your response: _____

7. I think my daughter's teacher is not doing enough to challenge her. I don't know what to do. If I suggest this to him, he may take offense and take it out on her.

   Response A: You should tell him what you think. He should listen to you.

   Your response: _____

8. It's about time they lifted the mandate for wearing masks. We are sick and tired of having to wear them.

   Response A: Yes, that's right. We're over the danger. Let's get back to normal.

   Your response: _____

9. My daughter tells me that she is feeling very stressed about school, about masks, about socializing with her friends. I don't know how to help her. Do you think I should get her to see a therapist?

   Response A: Just ignore it. She'll get over it.

   Your response: _____

10. My kids are spending a lot of time on social media. On the one hand, that's the way they connect with their peer groups. On the other hand, who knows what they are learning. What do you think I should do about it?

    Response A: You're right. Kids should get out and play more and get away from their tablets. I don't know what these kids are coming to.

    Your response: _____

11. I find it very difficult to talk with my son about certain topics that are probably important for him to understand. But I don't know how to approach him or if he would feel that I'm being intrusive.

    Response A: I know what you mean. My son is giving me the same problem.

    Your response: _____

12. My twins are making their college applications. They both want to go to Princeton, but I don't know if I can afford to send them if they don't get scholarships. I don't know what to do. I don't want to disappoint them, but should I mortgage my house to send them?

    Response A: Don't worry about it. It's not a disgrace if they have to go to a state college.

    Your response: _____

13. I think the last two years of living with the pandemic have changed all of us. And I'm not sure it's for the better.

> Response A: That can't be true. There's no basis for what you are saying. I think it's all in your mind.
>
> Your response: _____

14. I don't understand why the United States doesn't send troops to help the Ukrainians. We sent troops to Afghanistan and to Iraq. Surely the people there are just as deserving.

> Response A: Maybe Americans just don't want to be sucked into another war. We did our bit in Afghanistan and look how that ended.
>
> Your response: _____

15. You can't believe anything you read on social media. They just post these outrageous lies and expect people to respond. I think the Internet is malicious.

> Response A: Hey, not all of those posts are lies. There is some important stuff too.
>
> Your response: _____

16. The most important thing to her is how she looks, what she is wearing, and her hair style. How can I keep a friendship up with her when we have nothing more to talk about than appearances?

> Response A: Maybe you should just give her a break. She doesn't have to be like you or think like you to be your friend.
>
> Your response: _____

17. There are certain topics now that you just can't talk about with your family—especially when your family is divided about politics.

> Response A: Some families are like that. Mine is like that too.
>
> Your response: _____

18. My son locks the door to his room when he comes home from school, and after dinner. I don't know what he is doing in there. I don't want to pry—but I worry about him.

> Response A: That's what teenagers are like. Just ignore it.
>
> Your response: _____

19. My friend borrowed $200 from me a few months ago, she said to help her pay her phone bill. She hasn't returned it yet—and I don't know how to ask her about it without hurting her feelings.

> Response A: You should have known better than to lend money to people who are not going to pay it back.

Your response: _____

20. I've always been afraid to say what I think because I worry that people will think I'm not very smart. I've never even raised my hand in class.

    Response A: You're not stupid. You should try to get over it.
    Your response: _____

21. People think I'm cold and distant. I'm just not very sociable. Is that a crime?

    Response A: You should try to be more sociable. Then people would like you better you know.
    Your response: _____

22. I can't wait until we are free from having to wear masks and having to show a "passport" to go into a restaurant. All those restrictions are making me crazy.

    Response A: Don't feel that way. It will pass in time.
    Your response: _____

23. My dad has gotten very infirm now and he lives on his own. I think he should move into a care facility—you know, one of those retirement places where there are people who are available to take care of you if you need it. But he won't hear of it. He's as stubborn as a mule.

    Response A: Just leave him alone. Maybe he will come around eventually.
    Your response: _____

24. "I don't feel like going to school today. Do I have to go?"

    Response A: Yes, of course you have to go. School is not an option.
    Your response: _____

25. "I hate my life. I wish I was someone else."

    Response A: Snap out of it. Complaining will not help you.
    Your response: _____

SELF-EVALUATION OF YOUR RESPONSES

Use the Analyzing Responses in Human Discourse tool in the previous chapter to check on the alternate responses you made. Be especially attentive to how you were able to tune in to what the person is saying;

to your ability to remain neutral and non-judgmental; to your carefully phrased response, whether it was a paraphrase, asking for an example, or an interpretation.

As you review your responses, check to see that:

- Your response communicated respect for the other person's idea.
- You were able to free yourself from the need to evaluate the other person's idea.
- You were able to avoid commenting on the other person's idea reactively and/or offering your own opinion.
- You were able to make meaning of, to apprehend, what the other person was saying.
- Your response showed awareness of any affect that was being communicated.
- Your response accurately and sensitively reflected the meaning of the other person's statement.
- Your response had the best chance of making the other person feel safe, non-threatened, and non-defensive.

CONCLUSION

This task represents the second step in the development of your skills in these interpersonal dialogues. These beginning steps are the building blocks of what comes next: the more intense and more venturesome work of practice in live situations.

Remember: these skills are not mastered in two or three steps; these practice tasks are the mere beginning of what becomes a lifetime of work using and honing such skills, to the benefit of all of our human interactions. If the building of trust and respect in our human relationships is the goal, the work you do should be worth your best efforts.

25. (Adult to adult) There's still such discrimination toward women. Why do you think it's so hard for women to be accepted as political candidates?

    Your response: _____

    How the adult might reply: _____

SELF-EVALUATION OF YOUR RESPONSES

If you have been working with a friend, colleague, or partner, discussing the responses with each other is one way of making assessments of them.

Failing that, evaluation of one's own work can also lead to greater insights and point in the direction of additional understanding and skill development. In either case, use the criteria at the beginning of the chapter as a guide, as well as "Analyzing Responses in Human Discourse" in the chapter 7, to make your assessments of your responses.

One important indicator of the effectiveness of your responses is the way you perceive the child or adult in each situation to have replied to them. If their reply suggests that you have understood, that you have shown respect, that you have opened the dialogue for further discussion, these should be taken as indicators that your response has been helpful, and not hurtful, respectful and not judgmental, facilitative and not subtractive.

Once again, as you review your responses, check to see that:

- Your response communicated respect for the other person's idea.
- You were able to free yourself from the need to evaluate the other person's idea.
- You were able to avoid commenting on the other person's idea reactively and/or offering your own opinions.
- You were able to make meaning of, to apprehend, what the other person was saying.
- Your response showed awareness of any affect that was being communicated.
- Your response accurately and sensitively reflected the meaning of the other person's statement.

- Your response had the best chance of making the other person feel safe, non-threatened, and non-defensive.

CONCLUSION

This task represents the third step in the development of your skills as a facilitative responder. Your increased awareness and skill should now provide you with the means and the understanding to take on more challenging practice tasks.

Chapter 10

Creating Your Own Scenario

This task is a precursor to the more challenging "one-on-one" tasks that follow in subsequent chapters. In it, you create your own scenario, an extensive dialogue, to demonstrate your use of facilitative interpersonal skills in a pseudo-live discussion. In these scenarios, you are both the responder and the respondent.

Some topics are suggested below—but you should feel free to create your own topic, with the proviso that the more "heated" the issue, the more challenging the dialogue is likely to be.

And once again, when you have completed the task, you are asked to make some self-evaluations of your work, using "Analyzing Responses in Human Discourse" in chapter 7 to note the kind of responses you made and making an overall assessment of the conversation.

You may wish to choose a parent to child, or adult to adult dialogue. While one attempt at this task is suggested, practice creating additional scenarios will surely increase your knowledge and skill in the interpersonal process.

SUGGESTED TOPICS

1. Interpersonal issues with mates, siblings, relatives, parents, children
2. Current events
3. Issues that create stress in your life
4. Performance anxiety
5. Dietary issues
6. School or academic issues
7. Situations that have aroused anger

8. Worries about health, safety, illness
9. Social issues
10. Financial, economic issues
11. Injustice issues
12. Political issues
13. COVID/vaccination issues

In creating your scenario, remember to include at least a dozen or more responses that you, the responder, would make in the conversation. Include also the reply that you believe your response would generate in the person with whom you are having this conversation. Use the examples of conversations in chapter 7 as a guide in developing your own scenario.

Whether you do this on a tablet, your computer, or with pencil and paper, keep a record of your scenarios for further examination and analysis as you work to improve your skills in interpersonal dialogues.

SELF-EVALUATION OF YOUR CONVERSATION

Take a few days to distance yourself from the work you did in creating your scenario. Then, examine it with a fresh view of how you responded, and how your responses influenced what the respondent said in reply.

Use "Analyzing Responses in Human Discourse" in chapter 7 to make an analysis of each of your responses, noting whether each helped to build trust in the dialogue or whether each served to diminish trust. Note also the nature of each response so that you become more familiar with the different responses that build or diminish trust in human discourse.

When you have made your analyses of your responses, review the scenario again, and examine how the responses that build trust work to facilitate the replies made by the respondent and how the responses that diminish trust generate altogether different replies.

Make an overall assessment of your work as a responder in these scenarios, being especially attentive to the following:

1. What kinds of statements were more difficult for you to respond to?

2. What statements were easier?
3. What replies generated more emotionality for you?
4. What replies were easier for you?
5. What responses did you use more often than others?
6. What responses might you have used instead?
7. How did an inappropriate response create problems for the respondent in the scenario?
8. What do you need to keep in mind for your ongoing skill development?
9. In retrospect, how would you assess your responses as a way of building trust in your relationship with the respondent?
10. What overall assessment would you make of your ways of responding in this scenario? What criteria are you using to make this determination?

CONCLUSION

Now that you have created your first scenario, and made a self-assessment of your skill, start again and create a new scenario, this time being more attentive to what you have noted about your responses in the self-assessment, and try to make those improvements in the second conversation. Once again use "Analyzing Responses in Human Discourse" in chapter 7 to identify the responses you have made and complete the overall assessment as well.

This step in your skill development is the precursor for what comes next: practice in one-on-one conversations in real situations.

Chapter 11

One-on-One Practice in Attending and Responding with Respect (A)

Before beginning your one-on-one work to practice your conversation skills, it is helpful to remember some of the following conditions that enable your work in building trust in your human relationships. For this task, you will need a partner, a volunteer, who is amenable to participating in this dialogue.

Remember that your ability to attend thoughtfully and perceive accurately—that is, to apprehend,increases when the following conditions are present:

- You are able to make and hold eye contact with the respondent.
- You are able to listen and to communicate respect for the other person's ideas.
- You are able to free yourself from the need to evaluate the respondent's idea, in either tone or word.
- You are able to avoid commenting on the respondent's idea reactively and/or offering your own opinion.
- You are able to make meaning of—to apprehend—what the respondent is saying.
- You have an awareness of tone of affect (verbal or non-verbal) being communicated by the respondent.
- You are especially aware of indicators of stress being shown by the respondent.
- You can formulate responses that accurately and sensitively reflect the meaning of the respondent's statements.

- You are able to make the respondent feel safe, non-defensive, and non-threatened throughout the discussion.

PRE-CONDITIONS

Obviously, you will need a "mate"—a friend, colleague, partner, a willing volunteer, to participate in the process of this trial discussion. At the first, your respondent should be clear about the nature of the task you are embarking on and should be a willing and hopefully eager participant in helping you to practice your skills. It may be a good idea to introduce your respondent to the nature of the task before you begin, and the reason for your interest in furthering your skills in this area.

For this task, it is probably a better idea to choose an adult rather than a child—since this gives both of you the opportunity to participate in an informed, post-hoc assessment of the process.

Second, the topic or issue chosen by the respondent should be something of importance to him or her—the more real the issue, the more real the discussion. The respondent should be given a chance to identify that issue—something that has true meaning for him or her and something that he or she is willing to talk about.

Third, you will need to set up a quiet place for the discussion, one that is relatively free from interruptions, one that is comfortable for both parties.

Last, the person you have chosen to work with should be someone familiar, someone who already has a positive relationship with you, someone who cares about your developing skill in this area, in other words, an ally. Such a compadre would mean that there are no barriers between you, and that the pathway is open for a normal and true conversation.

TASK

In this task you practice the skills of attending, paraphrasing, interpreting, and asking for more information (e.g., Tell me more) as you respond to your partner in the process. Paraphrasing gives you a chance to "say back" the important aspects of the statement in some new way so that the respondent has a chance to hear it from a new perspective. Interpreting allows you to "read into" the respondent's statement, adding perhaps something more than he or she has said.

1. Use the list of issues (see chapter 10) if necessary, to give the respondent some ideas about a topic to discuss. The respondent should be free to choose a topic that has true meaning for him or her.
2. Ask the respondent to begin by making a statement about the issue.
3. Begin your responses by carefully attending to the statement, using paraphrasing, interpreting, or asking for more information, responses that you think appropriate. Remember to show interest, to be respectful, and to maintain a neutral position.
4. Allow the conversation to proceed to its natural conclusion.
5. Take a break!
6. Debrief the role play with both of you addressing the following questions from your perspective as well as from the respondent's.
   - To what extent were you able to attend to the respondent's issues?
   - To what extent were you able to capture the meaning of the respondent's statements accurately?
   - How did the respondent seem to react to your responses?
   - What were some difficulties you experienced in responding to these issues?
   - What were some difficulties, if any, experienced by the respondent?
   - How did your responses serve to build trust in the relationship?
   - How did your responses facilitate the respondent's deeper understanding of the issues?
   - What other comments can you and your compadre make about this practice session?
   - What comments can you add with respect to what you need to do to further develop your interactive skills?
7. Write your responses to this practice session in your ongoing journal.
8. Take several days to reflect on this experience. Then:
9. Find another "mate" and do the task again.

CONCLUSION

The keys to effective responding in interpersonal conversations lie in
your ability to attend, to respond respectfully, to invite the respondent to
reflect on his or her ideas, to pace the dialogue so the respondent feels
safe and unthreatened in offering their ideas. You also able to allow
the respondent time to reflect and time to formulate his or her ideas. In
reflecting on the responses you have made, you begin to perceive how
the respondent is able to use them to process, and to re-conceptualize
their ideas. Your appreciation of these conditions reflect your growing understanding of how best to promote the feelings of safety in a
conversation.

In all of your interactions, you are ever mindful of keeping the conversation "on track"—focusing on the aspects that are worth deeper
reflection and consideration. Being able to do that keeps the conversation centered on more important issues and away from trivia and
disconnected thoughts. When all of these occur, the dialogue is more
likely to build to deeper levels of trust and significant meaning in our
conversations.

Chapter 12

One-on-One Practice in Attending and Responding with Respect (B)

As you have no doubt noticed, each task in the self-instructional program is increasingly challenging, taking you one step further in your skill development. So while this task seems a repeat of the one in chapter 11, where you begin to work in one-on-one practice sessions, the two tasks in this chapter require you to record the practice sessions so that you can, in retrospect, listen to your responses as they actually played out in your conversation.

Most, if not all Smartphones have a voice recording device, and that tool is essential for these tasks. As well, you will again need a partner, a volunteer, who is willing to participate in this dialogue. You may, of course, ask the same person as you did for the previous task; however, it will broaden your experience if you ask someone else.

This task will be repeated twice. In the first practice session, it is suggested that you choose an adult as a participant. For the second practice, it is suggested that you ask a child to participate. These two different practice sessions will add to your experience as a responder in both adult to adult and adult to child conversations. Recording the two sessions will give you important data about your responses and help you identify your strengths and point to where you need further practices.

What follows is necessarily a repeat of the protocols for the previous task.

POINTS TO REMEMBER IN
INTERPERSONAL DISCUSSIONS

Remember that your ability to attend thoughtfully and perceive accurately, that is to apprehend, increases when the following conditions are met:

* You are able to make and hold eye contact.
* You are able to listen and to communicate respect for the other person's ideas.
* You are able to free yourself from the need to evaluate the ideas, in either tone or word.
* You are able to avoid commenting on the ideas and/or offering your own opinions.
* You are able to make meaning of, to apprehend, what is being said.
* You have an awareness of indicators of affect (verbal or non-verbal) being communicated.
* You are especially aware of signs of stress in evidence.
* You can formulate responses that accurately and sensitively reflect the substance of the statements.
* You are able to make the other person feel safe, non-defensive, and non-threatened throughout the discussions.
* You use questions infrequently and only when they are essential to further the conversation.

PRE-CONDITIONS

Once you have a volunteer who has agreed to participate in the conversation, several other pre-conditions should be observed:

1. The topic or issue chosen by the respondent should be something of importance to him or her. The more real the issue, the more real the discussion. The respondent should be given a chance to identify what he or she wants to talk about—something that has true meaning for him or her; something that he or she is willing to discuss.

2. You will need a quiet place for the discussion, one that is relatively free from interruptions, one that is comfortable for both parties.
3. The person you have chosen to work with you should be someone familiar, someone who already has a positive relationship with you, someone who cares about your developing skill in this area, in other words, an ally. Such a compadre would mean that there are no barriers between you and that the pathway is open for a normal and real conversation.
4. In the second practice session for this task, the child chosen should also meet the above criteria—that is, he or she should be a willing participant; should select his or her own topic that has interest for him or her; should be someone familiar, who knows you and who understands the reason for this practice.
5. Last, you will need to set up your Smartphone so that it will be available to record the practice session.

TASK

1. Set up the area where the conversation will take place. Set up the Smartphone to record the conversation.
2. Ask the respondent to select the topic or issue for discussion. The topic should have some relevance for him or her—something that he or she is concerned about.
3. Allow the respondent to begin the conversation. Concentrate on attending to the statements, using paraphrasing, or interpreting, or asking for more information, as you think appropriate. Be respectful and maintain a neutral position.
4. Allow the conversation to continue until it comes to a natural conclusion. Show appreciation to the respondent for his or her participation in the practice task.
5. Take a break!
6. When you are ready for your self-evaluation, listen to the recording you made of the conversation and use the "Coding Sheet" section at the end of the chapter to analyze your responses. (Note: you might want to print out a copy of the Coding Sheet [following page] for repeat use.)

7. After analyzing your responses, make an overall assessment of
   your work in this conversation. Be especially attentive to the
   following:
   • To what extent were you able to attend accurately to the respon-
     dent's statements?
   • To what extent were you able to apprehend the meanings of the
     respondent's statements?
   • How did the respondent seem to react to your responses?
   • What were some difficulties you experienced in the conversation?
   • What were some difficulties, if any, experienced by the
     respondent?
   • How did your responses serve to build trust in the relationship?
   • What other comments can you make about this conversation?
   • What do you need to do to further develop your skills?
8. Add your comments to the ongoing record of your work in
   your journal.
9. Take several days to reflect on this experience. Then, set up a sec-
   ond practice session with a child this time and do the task again.

CODING SHEET

Responses That Diminish Trust

1. Doesn't give the respondent a chance to finish the statements

_____

2. Agrees/disagrees with the statements

_____

3. Tells the respondent what s/he think

_____

4. Interrupts; talks too much; explains it his/her way

_____

5. Cuts the respondent off

_____

6. Shifts the discussion away from the respondent; tells what happened to him or her

_____

7. Heckles, is sarcastic, belittles the respondent's ideas

_____

8. Shames, humiliates, is offensive

_____

9. Gives advice; makes judgments about the statement or the person

_____

10. Puts the respondent on the defensive

_____

Responses That Build Trust

1. Expressly attends and tunes in to what is being said

_____

2. Accepts the respondent's statements/feelings no matter how off putting they may be

_____

3. Is non-defensive in responding

_____

4. Paraphrases statements with accuracy

_____

5. Makes effective interpretations of the statements

_____

6. Asks for more information (e.g., "tell me more") or examples to clarify a point being made

_____

7. Is reassuring in accepting what is being said

_____

8. Uses questions sparingly and appropriately

_____

9. Is respectful in word and in tone of voice

CONCLUSION

By now, you should have a growing understanding of how we build trust in our conversations, whether they occur with another adult, or with a child. You should also, by virtue of hearing yourself on the voice recording, have a clearer idea of your strengths in carrying out these conversations and the areas where you might still need additional practice. Having such personal awareness of your own skill development is a major factor in your progress, in not only these practice sessions, but also in real life situations. For most of us who use these skills, the art of learning to listen to oneself as one speaks is a lifelong challenge.

Before moving on to the next task in the self-instructional program, you might consider repeating the task in chapter 12 as many times as you think warranted, based on your own assessment of your work to date. While this may seem exhausting, consider what Andres Segovia told one of his students, when asked how he managed to perfect his guitar virtuosity, "My son," Segovia replied, "I practice my scales five hours every day."

Chapter 13

Practice in Attending and Responding (Encore)

Oh no! Not another repeat of the task in chapter 12!

Oh yes, with one additional wrinkle.

Use the information in chapter 12 to carry out one additional practice session with either child or adult and follow the protocols for carrying out the task. This time, upon completion, use the template below to make a verbatim transcript of your conversation.

Yes, this is a tedious job—listening to yourself, to the way your respondent replies to you, and to the way the conversation unfolds as you use your newly acquired conversation skills. But the truth is that nothing quite compares to seeing your words in print, and recognizing from those written elements your strengths and the areas of needed improvement. You can use whatever medium works best—computer, tablet, or pencil and paper for your transcript. But whatever medium, remember to include, at the end, your overall assessment of how the conversation evolved and how your responses facilitated the establishing of trust and respect.

The template below is easy to follow; but be sure to include, in the Alternate column, what you might have said instead, if your actual response seemed inappropriate. Use the Coding Sheet (chapter 12) as an aid in helping you identify your responses in the analysis column.

VERBATIM TRANSCRIPT TEMPLATE

Topic: _____

Respondent's Statement: _____

Your Response: _____

Analysis of Response: _____

Alternate: _____

CONCLUSION

In your overall evaluation of your conversation, see if you can get an overall sense of how your responses contributed to making your respondent feel at ease, comfortable, not defensive, and respected throughout. Determine which of your responses seem to have contributed to those conditions. See if you can tell which of your responses seem to have put the respondent on the defensive, made him or her angry, made him or her feel challenged, and under attack.

Once you have identified those "sore points," ask yourself what, in that conversation, did you say or do that provoked those more negative responses. And ask yourself what you might have done differently.

Then, armed with this increased knowledge of how you respond in interpersonal conversations, try this task again, with a new "mate"— either child or adult.

Chapter 14

Using Effective Interpersonal Skills in Real-Life Situations

There comes a time in every learner's life when he or she is ready to take that knowledge out of the classroom, or training center, into the real world. There comes a time in every piano student's life when she is ready to perform in front of an audience. There comes a time in every student teacher's practicum when he or she is ready to face own classroom.

Now that you have gone through the seven-step, self-instructional program in teaching yourself how to improve the way you talk to others, it is time for you to take your newly learned skills out into the "marketplace" of human discourse.

As you venture out into the field, you will, doubtless, come upon many opportunities to use your newly acquired skills in making conversation with others, adults, children, strangers, friends, or relatives. You won't have templates for Analyzing Responses in Human Discourse (chapter 7) and the Coding Sheet (chapter 12) at your fingertips; it's more like flying solo. You may, of course, stumble and retreat to earlier patterns of responding. But the more you proceed to invest yourself in using these interpersonal skills with others, the more you can reflect on how each conversation was facilitated by your responses, the more you will be gaining skill and the more skillful you will become.

Most important is for you to be continually tuned in to what is coming out of your mouth—so you are not deceived in believing that you are respectful when, in fact, you are not. Most important is for you to be continually aware of how your responses contribute to the feelings of trust engendered in the dialogue with your respondent.

This is a lifelong process and one that only you can decide on its value to you. As you proceed in this lifelong journey, don't neglect to keep your journal current—keeping track of your conversations, how each was enabled by your responses, how each respondent reacted, how you were able to show respect and build trust in the relationship. And where your "triggers" were—what topics or issues made it more difficult for you to be neutral and not become angry or defensive. These insights into self can only occur when you have shed any defenses about the way you talk to others, keeping open the pathway for increased mastery of your skills.

Chapter 15

Last Words

As you bring your preparatory work to a conclusion, there are, at least, two important questions that you need to ask yourself. One is: Why on earth should I spend my time learning these skills? The second is: Does this self-instructional program work? (In other words, if I devote my time to these studies, will my interpersonal conversation skills improve?) These questions and others are addressed in these last words of this book.

In her recent book, *I Never Thought of It That Way: How to Have Fearlessly Curious Conversations in Dangerously Divided Times*, Monica Guzman (2022) writes that we now live in a broken world in which divergent viewpoints preclude relationships. "Rejecting someone for their class, race, or sexual orientation still remains taboo, but dissing people, threatening, or shaming them for their political beliefs, is the ultimate virtual signaling." Guzman's big idea is that one should give up the need to be right and instead focus on the need to stay connected; that such connections will enrich us.

It is, at the bottom line, a matter of what you believe is important in your life—to be able to make these human connections, with the hope that each one enriches us, or if you are content to stand aside, or stand back, while the schisms in our lives continue to widen. Yes, at the end, it's a matter of what you consider important; whether to take a stand to make a difference or to stand back and disengage. Yes, it's a big ask: to consider the way we interact with each other and how to improve those human relationships. How important is this to me?

No one can answer that question other than oneself.

You might well ask, "What's the payoff?" So what if I believe in the importance of building these human connections. What's in it for me?

This is not a TV program where you win a prize if your interpersonal skills improve. You are not promised a seat at God's table in the next life. You don't get a gold star, or a lifetime achievement award. In short, there are no concrete payoffs in material terms. There is only the satisfaction of having the skills to do something helpful, wise, and important that no one else might appreciate other than yourself as you see yourself mastering these important skills.

One has to ask oneself whether improving our human connections is important to us; whether it will improve the quality of life of those with whom we interact and in doing so, improve the quality of our own lives. Will each positive conversation, each more human connection, make a significant difference in the quality of our own lives? Some of us think so.

There is one further benefit. As you continue to develop and master the skills that make for improved human conversations, eventually you become that person—the person whose ways of responding is now who you are. There is a lot of self-satisfaction in being authentically that person.

Some may quibble: "I'm too old to change; I'm too deeply rooted in my ways to change." That is one way of shutting the door to any improvement, a thin excuse for not having to take responsibility for what we are like. But change and improvement begins with one tiny step and with each succeeding step, it grows and blossoms until you have become one whose skills are so successfully integrated that you are able to use them without deliberate, conscious effort.

Again, only you can decide if it's worth it; if it's important; if this is something you want for yourself.

The second question has an easier answer. The steps in the self-instructional program have not been recently invented. The roots lie in the early work of Charles Truax (1967), Robert Carkhuff (1967), and Bernard Berenson (1967), to name a few who began work in interpersonal skills training. Similar programs were developed and used in the pre-service training of teachers at Simon Fraser University (Wassermann, 2017). The successes of these programs have been attested to by the various people who have benefited from them, over these many years.

Of course, benefits can only come about as each learner in the process gives the practice the attention and the commitment it requires to move from rudimentary beginnings to increased expertise. In other words, in a small edit from the acronym, WYSIWYG—WYPIIWYTO: What you put in is what you take out.

JUST ONE MORE THING

Despite having gone the long road in mastering these interpersonal skills, there will be times in one's life when certain conversations will defeat us; will make us angry, distressed, disappointed, disgusted— emotional responses that are triggered by someone, even someone close, who is making statements that, with all of your skills, make it impossible for you to respond respectfully. Yes, Virginia, we all have those tipping points. And for some of us, there may be no way around them; no way for us to respond respectfully in the face of utterances that make us crazy.

So what's the answer? How does one respond to statements that are absurd, that are full of venom, that are based on disinformation, that are racist or sexist, and go beyond anything that is rational? How does one overcome one's emotional "hot buttons" and respond respectfully?

To that question there is no easy answer. But it begins with knowing which topics and which statements press upon those "hot buttons" for you and stepping back from any kind of response. In other words, if you can't be authentic and respectful in your responses, it's best to retreat and not engage, as any disrespectful response will only exacerbate the situation. It takes a great deal of sympathy and a great deal of self-possession to respond effectively in the presence of statements that go against the grain.

But if you can master that sympathy and self-possession and respond respectfully to even the most hair-raising statements, you are in a much better position to enhance that human connection. If not, there is not only no shame in that, but a real gain in self-awareness.

Bibliography

Berenson, Bernard & Carkhuff, Robert R. (1967). *The Sources of Gain in Counseling and Therapy.* New York: Holt, Rinehart and Winston.

Brooks, David (2022). "Dissenters Trying to Save Evangelicalism." *New York Times*, February 6, 2022, pp. 4–5.

Carkhuff, Robert R. (1969). *Helping and Human Relations, Volume II.* New York: Holt, Rinehart.

Carkhuff, Robert R. (2000). *The Art of Helping.* Amherst, MA: Human Resource Development Press.

Carkhuff, Robert R. & Berenson, Bernard G. (1967). *Beyond Counselling and Therapy.* New York: Holt, Rinehart and Winston.

Combs, Arthur & Syngg, Donald (1951). *Individual Behavior.* New York: Harper & Row.

Fisher, Roger & Ury, William (2012). *Getting to Yes.* New York: Random House.

Friere, Paolo (1983). *Pedagogy of the Oppressed.* London: Continuum.

Guzman, Monica (2022). *I Never Thought of It That Way: How to Have Fearlessly Curious Conversations in Dangerously Divided Times.* Dallas, TX: Ben Bella.

Homans, Charles (2022). "Where Does American Democracy Go from Here?" *New York Times*, March 20, 2022, pp. 28–49.

Kyle, Arnold (2014). "Behind the Mirror: Reflective Listening and Its Tain in the Work of Carl Rogers." *The Humanistic Psychologist*, 42(4), 354–369.

Lansbury, Janet (2022). "What If We Respected Toddlers as Whole People?" *New York Times*, February 15, 2022.

Leonard, Herman B. (1991). "With Open Ears: Listening and the Art of Discussion Leadership." In C. R. Christensen, David A. Garvin, & A. Sweet (eds.), *Education for Judgment: The Artistry of Discussion Leadership.* Boston: Harvard Business School Press.

Lyall, Sarah (2022). "We'd Like to Speak to the Manager." *New York Times*, January 2, 2022.

New York Times (2022). "Free Speech Is Under Threat," March 20, 2022, *Sunday Review Editorial*.

Rogers, Carl (1965). *Client Centered Therapy*. Cambridge, MA. Riverside Press.

Strauss, Valerie & Bever, Lindsey (2022). "Florida Rejects Math Books with References to Critical Race Theory." In *The Washington Post*, April 16, 2022.

Truax, Charles B. & Carkhuff, Robert R. (1967). *Toward Effective Counseling and Psychotherapy*. Chicago: Aldine Publishing.

Wassermann, Selma (1994). *Introduction to Case Method Teaching: A Guide to the Galaxy*. New York: Teachers College Press.

Wassermann, Selma (2017). *The Art of Interactive Teaching*. New York: Routledge.

Wassermann, Selma (2021). *Mastering the Art of Teaching*. Lanham, MD: Rowman & Littlefield.

Zenger, Jack & Folkman, Joseph (2016). "What Great Listeners Actually Do." *Harvard Business Review*, July 14, 2016. https://hbr.org/product/what-great-listeners-actually-co/HO30DC-PDF-ENG

About the Author

Selma Wassermann is a Professor Emerita in the Faculty of Education at Simon Fraser University. She is the recipient of the University Award for Teaching Excellence. Her nineteen previous books include *Mastering the Art of Teaching* (2021), *Opening Minds* (2021), *Evaluation without Tears* (2020), *What's the Right Thing to Do* (2019), *Teaching for Thinking Today* (2009), and *Case Method Teaching: A Guide to the Galaxy* (1994).